CONTRACTS FOR
Difference

MASTER THE TRADING REVOLUTION

CATHERINE DAVEY

Wrightbooks

First published 2003 by Wrightbooks
an imprint of John Wiley & Sons Australia, Ltd
42 McDougall Street, Milton, Qld 4064
Office also in Melbourne

Typeset in Goudy 11.5/13.8 pt

Reprinted May 2004, January 2005, December 2005, September 2006,
June 2007 and April 2009

The moral rights of the author have been asserted

National Library of Australia Cataloguing-in-Publication data:

Davey, Catherine

Contracts for difference: master the trading revolution

Includes index

ISBN 0 7314 0026 7

1. Futures. 2. Stocks – Prices 3. Stock options
   I. Title

332.6322

Some material contained in this book has appeared on the InvestorWeb Research site (www.investorweb.com.au). This material is reproduced here with permission.

Please note that the company referred to throughout this book as **CMC Group** is now known as **CMC Markets**.

Cover design by Rob Cowpe

Author photo by Alex Craig

Printed in Australia by McPherson's Printing Group

10 9 8 7

Disclaimer

CONTENTS

Christopher Tate (author of *The Art of Trading*) on CFDs:

The internet revolution brought about many changes in the way traders did business. However, the fundamental relationship between broker and client stayed largely unchanged; you paid the broker for the privilege of executing your orders. For this payment you often got reams of useless research but very rarely anything of value such as the ability to set stop-loss orders electronically or the ability to trade a variety of markets from a single platform.

The emergence of contracts for difference and groups such as CMC Group has changed this relationship on a fundamental level. In an interesting conundrum the cost of doing business has been reduced but the range of services that are offered has increased. Stop-losses, contingent orders and the ability to trade multiple markets are now standard features for traders...as the most interesting new product to hit the market CFDs have reinvigorated my interest in designing new trading systems to take advantage of their unique features.

FOREWORD BY
DAVID TREW

CMC Markets

My introduction to the CFD market came at the beginning of the year 2000, when CMC Markets, my employer, launched contracts for difference for retail traders as a commission-free product in the UK. CMC was a far cry from my days working for the likes of The First National Bank of Chicago and Republic National Bank of New York. Prior to joining CMC I had traded for institutions in the foreign exchange and precious metals markets. In fact, it was with some unease I swapped my safe banking career for a job on the retail side of the markets. Thankfully I caught the wave at exactly the right moment and am privileged to have been a part of a watershed product that has truly been a revolution for private traders.

As one of the first CFD providers in the UK, I was able to witness first-hand the almost immediate popularity of CFDs.

Clients liked the idea of leverage, but one of the main drivers of the popularity of CFDs in those days was the ability to avoid stamp duty in the UK. Clients could now get the same access to the sharemarket as traditional share dealing through their stock broker, but could avoid the 0.5 per cent stamp duty on each position that derivative trades were exempt from.

As everyone now knows 1999 to 2000 were heady times for stock markets all around the world. Technology stocks in particular were booming, the Nasdaq reached record levels at 6,500 and the Dow topped at 11,500. A lot of hot money was flowing through the system and for many it was not a case of skill but a case of buy, buy, buy to obtain substantial profits. Any dips in the local market were seen as buying opportunities.

Hence, it was stamp duty and leverage that fuelled the initial popularity of this product during the rampant bull market, referred to by Alan Greenspan as 'irrational exuberance'. Looking back, it was a great time for investors, advisers and brokers alike.

The day I met Peter Cruddas, the founder of CMC, for my initial job interview, he told me two things that seemed like typical employer hype. He said the retail brokering market was going to change forever and this job would be one of the best of my life. So far he's been right.

The first thing that struck me when I joined CMC was the sheer size of the business going through the company. The volume of trades rivalled the interbank market. I was also surprised by the size of individual accounts and the large trades these individuals made—the kinds of positions I was accustomed to seeing institutional traders take.

Cruddas was a legendary institutional foreign exchange (FX) trader before he established CMC. He used his understanding of the FX market and trading to offer leveraged (margin) foreign exchange trading to private clients. His formula was narrow spreads and no transaction costs. The pricing of the margin FX product was so competitive, there were soon banks and brokers using the service.

When Cruddas decided CMC should enter the CFD market he took all the good points of the margin FX product and applied it to the equity market. He believed there was a better way than simply brokering equity trades and settling them as CFDs, which was really just acting as a toll booth for market access like any other broker. With his vision and mantra of 'give the clients what they want!' he opened the floodgates to what has literally become a trading revolution.

Market making, as opposed to broking, changed the landscape of CFD trading. Because clients could deal on share prices without having to physically settle the trade, the clearing, settlement and taxation expenses of the underlying market were now irrelevant. Market makers could more efficiently manage their books using proxy hedges and matching trades to lower the cost of market access. Such techniques became mere operational expenses and, as such, there was nothing to pass on to the client.

Savvy investors took the 'easy money' of the bull market, leveraged it, went short earning the interest yield, wore some P&L swings, and stuck to their guns. One morning after the Dow had fallen over 200 points, we had a customer who started shorting anything on the UK market he could get his mouse on. He had shorted over 60 FTSE100 stocks in the first three minutes before he moved on to the European markets. The trader was a professional with a very large appetite for risk and a well funded account. It looked like the move he had been stalking was about to pay off.

Spreads were wide and the market had gapped lower. He was taking an extremely risky strategy and probably breaking every rule of every book on trading. In the volatile weeks before he shorted the market, almost every major broadsheet in London had run a story on sitting tight and riding out the storm sweeping the world's stock markets. Repeatedly Bloomberg and CNBC broadcast American analysts seeing 'value' in the US economy. This trader took all that information and hurled it out the window of his home dealing room in those three minutes.

After the initial flurry, the market quietened ahead of the US market open and his position looked hairy. Fortunately, when the US opened, investor confidence, still shaken, pushed the market lower, and the client started to make a huge amount of money.

Speed, access and leverage enabled this bold customer to make amazing profits, and it was CFDs that allowed him to do it.

This dramatic event was to prove the forerunner to a bear market where we saw the number of our clients taking short positions on stocks and stock indices grow astronomically. Some months after this dramatic act of shorting we saw markets in the US and Europe capitulate to large program trades as portfolio managers dumped stock. Positive stock analysts became harder to find, and the retail market becomes more cynical as negative fund performance hits almost everyone with retirement savings.

As director of trading for CMC Markets I have seen the birth, growth, maturity, and continued expansion of off-exchange derivative trading from its beginnings in the UK, as it sweeps the world. CFDs are a powerful product with benefits previously unavailable to many private clients who have an interest in the stock market. I have seen clients make equity CFD trades for as little as one share CFD per trade—a common alternative to paper trading and a great way to dip your toe in the water—to index trades as large as US$115 million per transaction. The popularity of CFDs will continue to climb regardless of the underlying conditions of the market or economy because they allow you to trade cheaply in any direction.

CFDs are not a new concept. They have been traded in the institutional market for around two decades, otherwise referred to as equity swaps. They allow large fund managers to quickly and cost-effectively hedge both individual and entire exposures across their portfolios. You can also trade CFDs on equity indices. Contracts such as the Dow Jones Industrial Average, the Financial Times Stock Exchange (FTSE) 100 or, in Australia, the Share Price Index (SPI) contract all offer the opportunity to exchange the difference in cash between your buy price and your sell price in the same way as a CFD.

CFDs are theoretically possible on almost any asset or market that moves. CFDs on shares are the most popular, followed by stock market indices, foreign exchange and metals. They are particularly popular on gold and silver with our clients in the Middle East. Wealthy sheiks have taken positions on gold into the tens of millions of dollars and hold them for months and even years, through thick and thin. Asian and East European clients favour the increased leverage and non-stop action of the foreign exchange and equity market. The populatrity of CFDs has meant our UK operation has built a worldwide client base without having to set-up a single regional office—until now.

Australia is our first foray outside the UK and the response to CFDs already looks set to surpass our UK experience.

Some people might say the word 'revolution' is too strong in describing the CFD phenomenon, but I stand by these words.

CFDs are a trading revolution because no other derivative trading product has been met with such extraordinary global demand—a demand that is driven by a range of attributes that previously only institutional investors had access to.

Welcome to the revolution!

I'VE DONE ALL THE DUMB THINGS

A few years ago I saw Kylie Minogue interviewed on the *60 Minutes* television show. She described the day she went to a literary conference at Albert Hall in London, attended by Britain's intellectual elite.

At the conference she stood up and recited the words of her early hit song *I Should Be So Lucky*, without the music. Minogue's aim was to revisit her past; for the permed and suburban Kylie to be exorcised forever. She said the experience was difficult but nevertheless a watershed.

In this chapter I would like to exorcise the demons of my trading past by recounting my version of *I Should Be So Lucky*. I will tell you the story of how I got into the trading business, because I know my story is probably not that different from many small traders' first encounters with the market.

Ironically, being lucky is the exact opposite of my story. In fact, I borrow from the chorus of another popular Australian song when I call this story 'I've Done All the Dumb Things'.

No.1 Dumb Thing

My first experience of the trading business was in 1989. I had graduated from a communications degree where I had topped the class in accounting and achieved mediocre results in every other subject.

The rest of my classmates went on to become journalists and advertising executives. Instead, I watched the movie *Wall Street* and thought the character Bud Fox was handsome so I decided I would like to get a job in trading.

This was the 'No.1 dumb thing'—I thought trading was a glamorous business.

I got a job as a brokers' assistant at one of the biggest futures brokers in Sydney at the time. An important task of the day was to fetch breakfast. By the end of the first week, the manager of the retail brokering desk, without any qualm or joke intended, called me the waitress. These were the days before a girl could get litigious about such comments.

It was also the days of hand-drawn charts—so I spent a lot of my day updating every local and international futures contract by hand. I don't remember any of the brokers really looking at these charts. My boss was an ex-pat American who picked his nose in full view of the office. The most exciting day was when two of the brokers had a punch-up. I lasted five months.

No.2 Dumb Thing

Five years later the futures business came back into my life when I was living in London. I was sharing a house with a bunch of Australians and one of them was a guy who had an unusual dream. He wanted to spend his summers surfing and the winters snowboarding. This wasn't an unusual aspiration for an early-20s Australian male, except that he planned to support this lifestyle by trading his own account.

When he told me his plan I thought, 'that sounds great, I want to do that too'.

This was the 'No.2 dumb thing'—I let greed rule my life.

The thing about greed is it makes the impossible seem realistic. After listening to my surfing friend rave about all the money to be made trading futures, I got busy saving my money so that I could quit my well-paid city job to be a full-time futures trader.

No.3 Dumb Thing

It took me about a year to save my money. During this time, I got busy reading books. I found a catalogue called 'Traders Press', which some of you may be familiar with. It has a great range of books, with good explanations.

At this stage I knew no-one else in the business of futures trading except my friend the surfer who ended up leaving town and never following his dream.

Looking through the 'Traders Press' catalogue, I found a range of books by one particular author that mentioned concepts like astro-trading, Gann and Elliott. I figured that trading was quite tricky, so therefore I was going to need to read some pretty clever books. I sent away for the most complicated-sounding books in the catalogue.

This brings me to 'No.3 dumb thing'—if it sounds complicated it will help you make money.

Complicated things serve a few destructive purposes in the trading world:

1   Complicated strategies give us a false sense of confidence that we are outsmarting the rest of the market.

2   Complicated strategies can never be fully understood, so they enable us to blame the system rather than ourselves.

3   Complicated systems require a lot of time and effort to understand and are therefore perfect for the procrastination factor—'I can't pull the trigger because my extremely complicated system hasn't given me all the signals.'

The process of becoming a good trader consists of three levels. And this is a quick test to see where you are on the curve. What do you think is most important and/or most challenging about trading?:

1   **Finding the right trades and entering the trade?** If you are new to the game then you are probably still grappling with finding the good trades.

2   **Exiting the trade and taking the profit?** If you are some ways down the track then your exits are most likely your main concern—for example, when do you let your profits run, when do you cut your losses?

3   **Deciding how much money to risk or money management?** If you are really getting on top of this trading lark then the most important factor for you is your money management—for example, when do you scale down your exposure, when do you bet big?

Complex systems will have you at stage 1 for a very long time, because you never have a watertight set of rules to analyse the market.

Anyway, back to my story.

No.4 Dumb Thing

Not content with the extremely complicated books (which in hindsight I realise were deliberately written in a cryptic fashion), I called the author and discussed the possibility of him giving me some tuition. I paid US$1,000 for this tuition.

I was living in London and he was living in the US. I would send him a question via fax. He would respond by asking me what I thought. Or worse still, I would fax him a chart of a market before it opened with a trade idea. He would call me after the market had opened and the opportunity had gone to tell me it was a good idea and he had jumped on the trade.

This brings me to 'No.4 dumb thing'—if it costs a lot it's good.

For US$1,000 I had three phone conversations and a couple of faxed communications. Small traders think if a book costs $150 or a course costs $1,000 it is going to be better than the $50 book or the $250 seminar. In fact, in some cases the high pricing of trading courses is just a smart marketing strategy in itself.

As a broker, I offered plenty of free seminars. You get lots of people attending who have an expectation that they won't learn anything particularly useful because it's free. If you go to a seminar that has a big five-digit price tag, then your expectation is you will be told something great. Many times all the speaker offers is a range of standard indicators available in any trading textbook.

No.5 Dumb Thing

Despite having entered the world of futures, being called a waitress and witnessing two brokers have a punch-up, I decided to start trading on the advice of a guy whose dream was to be a drop-out. I had spent a lot of money on books that talked about stuff like the 'Egg of Columbus', geometric means, and Mercury conjunct Venus. Finally, I'd blown US$1,000 on a couple of phone calls and a few faxes. I'd say there are quite a few of you who have a similar story to tell or who are even in the middle of that journey right now.

Maybe you have a different book collection, or have paid big dollars for a speaker in a better suit. But has this person helped you make a fortune?

The next thing I did was quit my job and trade full-time. With the abysmal resources I've just mentioned, I hoped to turn my meagre £5,000 (or about AUD$12,000 in local currency terms) into a fortune.

This is what actually happened. For the first month I went through the typical trading roller-coaster—a few wins then losses—but I managed to breakeven. Now, living in London plus the office space I was hiring, plus the costs of live data at that time because I was an intraday Treasury bond trader, added up to about £1,800 per month. So, even though I wasn't losing any money trading, the whole deal was costing me a fortune.

By the end of the third month, I had to quit. Not because I had lost my initial stake. In fact, I was up quite significantly through a process of simplifying my strategy and using some basic rules but, because I had gone through my cash reserves just living, I needed my initial stake to pay the bills.

So this brings me to 'No.5 dumb thing'—thinking you can turn a small amount of money into a fortune overnight.

In all the years I had been in the business of futures brokering, I never saw or heard of any new trader turning $10,000 into a fortune.

No.6 Dumb Thing

Not satisfied with the inevitable ending to my trading, I went back to working in the real world to save more money to return to trading. I came home to Australia and thought the best stepping stone to trading my own account was to return to broking. I expected futures broking in the late 1990s to be a more civilised environment than the late 1980s.

I was proved wrong. In the late 1990s the other side of the futures desk was still not much better than 'cowboy' town. I saw brokers breaking phones, regularly on the verge of fisty cuffs, more unsavoury habits I can't talk about, and sexism in the office that had definitely not evolved since the 1980s.

It was against the rules for registered representatives to trade their own account so I had to get special dispensation to do it. Since I was working full-time, and it was necessary for me to get another broker on the desk to execute my trades, I decided to follow a couple of the trading systems that the other brokers were managing for their clients. The two that were popular at the time were a gap system on the Nikkei and a system from a US dealer that was based on a percentage break-out strategy.

The Nikkei system that had been performing reasonably well before I started to trade it immediately started to take a nose dive as soon as I had made my first trade. I think I had about one winning trade in fifteen. The other system was devised by a US trader who was later investigated by the Securities and Exchange Commission (SEC) and was fined several millions of dollars. The only winning trade I had with that system was a trade where the night dealers had forgotten to execute the stop-loss.

This brings me to 'No.6 dumb thing'—there is someone else out there who knows more than I do and they can tell me how to do it.

This is possibly the biggest lesson of trading. When someone tells you they have the secret, don't believe them. This doesn't mean all the other authors or teachers out there are wrong. I just believe that trading is a highly personal journey. There are many, many ways to make money trading. That's the paradox—we are all running around looking for the 'Holy Grail', but the best system is the one you have found yourself. This means making the effort to study and research the markets.

When I talk about effort I don't mean wrapping yourself up in a complicated system that you will never truly grasp. Instead, it is about finding a system that suits you and then testing, researching, refining and formulating an individualised strategy that you can execute with 100 per cent confidence.

The big question is, how do you sift through all the stuff that's around and find the right one for you?

The answer is to go for what feels right. Forget about the complicated or mystical, or that some big fund manager swears by it. This is the stage in the process of becoming a successful trader where you really have to get in touch with your feelings. Go with what feels right, not what your head tells you should work. If it doesn't turn you on, ignore it.

For instance, if Elliott Wave theory gets you excited, but you get bogged down in wave counts, just use the Elliott information that works for you. I studied Elliott for a while and tried to get my head around irregulars and flats and a-b-c's. After all this study, the only theory I regularly use of Elliott Wave is how to identify wave one of a bull run. However, this doesn't mean Elliott Wave theory taken to the extreme doesn't work. One particular client from my futures brokering days was a consistently profitable trader and he was an Elliott Wave specialist. His style was to take huge drawdowns—maybe $2,000 on one lot of the index, but he never had a losing trade.

Now, the last instalment in my 'dumb' trading career was to actually hand over quite a significant amount of money to a friend who I thought was a good trader. I gave him the money on Friday, and went away for a holiday interstate. I didn't have any idea what the markets did that week, but when I got back to town I had $44 left in my account. I would like to say it was someone else's fault, but there was no-one to blame but me. The guy talked big, he was a friend, and I thought he knew what he was doing.

Avoiding the Dumb Things

As a broker, I have witnessed on a daily basis every dumb thing that can be done, most of which I have done myself at some stage. But there are a couple of key points that I have had the privilege to witness that I think are the difference between being a punter and a serious player:

↳ **Do the work**—there are absolutely, categorically no short-cuts to becoming a profitable trader. If you think successful traders have some special secret and it comes naturally to them, think again. The ones who make it know their stuff inside out and back to front. They go the extra mile. They spend the time. They don't take two minutes looking at a market, or worse still listening to someone else and deciding to trade. They have all the bases covered, so they expect to make money, but they are also able to identify instantly when they are wrong and get out. Do the work, do the work, do the work.

↳ **Keep your own counsel**—I want to stress how important this is. When I was a broker I realised the profitable clients are the ones who had absolutely no interest in my opinion. The popular opinion is usually wrong. Statistics show that only a small percentage of investors make money from trading their own account. I didn't really believe this until I became a broker and found the business depressing, because so many clients lost money. The key is to avoid becoming a statistic. You become a statistic by going around asking all the other statistics for their opinion. Reading the newspapers is a good way to become a statistic.

I have a pet theory about trading: how you approach the process of trading is exactly the same way you approach life generally.

You might be reading this book because you have been struggling to make money and you are hoping CFDs are the answer. If you want to know why you aren't a successful trader you just have to look at your strategy for dealing with any other important situation in your life.

The Roadmap to CFDs

Let me give you an example from my own life. One day I had to drive to Stanwell Tops, about an hour and a half away from Sydney. I was really excited to go, because at the other end I would have a great time with friends and this is a really nice place to be. My initial thought was, 'great, I can't wait to get there.' But then the next stage in my thought process went something like this: 'I am not from Sydney, and I really don't venture much out of the Eastern suburbs. I can't even go to the North Shore without consulting the street guide, and I suffer from the scourge that afflicts many modern women—I can't read a map.'

At the time, my car was a very small, unreliable model from the mid-1980s, with a top speed of about 80 kilometres per hour. I was really keen to go to Stanwell Tops, but I was also a hopeless and frustrated navigator in a car that was less than adequate for the journey.

I started the journey leaving a reasonable amount of time before I was due at Stanwell Tops. As I drove away from my home I noticed the car needed fuel and realised that a pit stop would likely put me behind schedule.

I hit the highway and was going OK until I had to turn off. This is where the map reading came into play. I started to consult the street directory and, of course, it was hopeless.

I gave up and called the people I was meeting up with and they gave me directions. Now, generally speaking, when I listen to someone else's directions I get even more confused (although the advantage is, when I do arrive and I'm hopelessly late, I can blame someone else).

I drove on for another half an hour and eventually called the people I was to meet again and discovered I had gone so far away, they didn't even recognise the landmarks I was describing to them. At this point I was thinking—and I might have even threatened to these friends—that I had had enough and was going to just turn around and go home. It all seemed too hard.

However, I regained my reason and, knowing that I was going in the wrong direction, I turned around and started driving back in the general direction of where I wanted to be. Quite suddenly, I came across a funny little wooded lane I had noticed on my way past the first time, but I thought to myself, 'that can't be it, it's too straightforward. I'm sure the route has a lot more turns.' It turned out to be the street where I was meant to be. I turned into the street and I saw my friends outside their house. Finally, I had arrived, and it felt like I had fluked it.

How does this winding story about me going to Stanwell Tops relate to trading? Well, this story is a good analogy for my trading journey.

Initially, I was enthusiastic, so I made a commitment to do it without really considering the challenges involved in trading. As I went along, I realised I may need some skills to make it happen.

I started to buy trading books. But, rather than choose the basic texts that would have given me the proven tools and an easier route to success, I went straight for the complex stuff that is frustrating and yields very little useful information.

I didn't take the easy turn-off, I kept going down the road looking for the complicated route.

So, I began my trading career by getting confused, losing money and not knowing how to make it work. In the midst of all this I actually went past the right path—which was at the beginning of my trading career when I traded full-time, went back to the basics and was making money.

Driving on, and feeling lost, I turned to someone I thought should know how to do it. Now, the problem with getting direction from friends is that they have their own perceptions of the way the world is so their directions are not necessarily right for me. I lost my way again—in fact I went in completely the wrong direction. Asking friends for directions was like giving my money to someone else to trade.

At this point I was considering if I even wanted to go to Stanwell Tops—how badly did I want to be a trader? But I don't like to give up when I've come so far and gone through so much pain. So I went back and tried to find my way. And this time, just when on the verge of giving up, I made it.

A New Consciousness

The Stanwell Tops story represents my unconscious strategy for life. Confronted with any new endeavour, going through all that rigmarole is what I do instinctively. Thinking about the experience made me realise many aspects of my life have followed a similar path.

I regret to say a lot of my relationships have taken on a similar pattern, as have the jobs I've undertaken and even my ability to master something physical. For example, I decided to take up in-line skating. I started out with the most expensive pair of skates I could find. I quickly discovered that these skates were expensive for a reason—they were fast. When I discovered that skating is quite difficult and even dangerous, those skates sat in the cupboard for about two years. Then, determined not to waste my investment, I found a good skater to show me the basics. In the process I broke three fingers, put myself through a lot of pain and was on the verge of giving up. But then, I simply allowed myself to enjoy it and I became a competent in-line skater.

My strategy for life was an unconscious one. Now that I have chosen to realise that unconscious strategy, I don't have to keep taking the wrong turns, breaking fingers or losing a lot of money to get where I want to go. Instead, I can consciously decide that my journey will be well prepared, as smooth as possible and with few U-turns.

What would have happened if I had looked at my street directory before I set out on my journey to Stanwell Tops and had the route clearly mapped out? What if I had left home half an hour earlier to get fuel, or better still, purchased fuel the day before? I would have saved myself a lot of pain and frustration during the journey and I would have arrived much sooner.

What unconscious pattern are you running in your life? How does it manifest in your trading? Do you like to do things at the last minute, or are you so cautious that you have trouble moving forward with anything you do? Are you put off by criticism, or do you consciously seek out approval from others to feel better about the decisions you make? I believe the process of deconstructing these unconscious patterns is an essential part of a trader's journey.

The Psychology of Trading

The psychology of trading is far more important than the strategy. When you hear of people who have the right temperament to trade, that they are naturals, you are really just hearing about people who have an unconscious strategy in life that happens to work with trading.

Trading is one of the most wonderful and frightening endeavours you can undertake. I guarantee it will be one of the biggest emotional challenges you can encounter in everyday life. Nothing is more formidable, more exciting, or takes you on such an in-depth journey into yourself. You can enter and exit a market in a day and make the equivalent of a weekly or monthly wage. An average person's daily salary can be made in the first 10 minutes of trading. Once bitten with the trading bug, you will find it impossible not to harbour the dream of one day trading full-time for a living.

Where you start on this trading journey is not where you will end. The path is the hero's journey. There will be moments when you are drawn to tears. And yes, in the beginning, I had a moment when I was in tears on the phone to my broker. There will be other moments when you will want to punch the air like a character from some cheesy American film. There are few other undertakings that will take you to the extremes of your emotions. The old saying 'what doesn't kill you only makes you stronger' applies to the trading journey. A month, a year, or a decade from now you will look back and be amazed at the depth of your knowledge of the markets and life you have acquired, regardless of what stage you are at with your trading when you read this book.

If I had my time over there wouldn't be much I'd change. Every loss taught me a lesson. There is one piece of advice I wish I had known back then and that is—'it's all OK':

- ↳ Losing money is part of the process and is OK.
- ↳ Making money and wanting to tell everybody is OK.
- ↳ Being wrong is OK.

The experience of trading places your human frailties under a 1,000 watt spot light. What is left is a very important life lesson. Being wrong or right, making money or losing it is part of the process and not who you really are. The psychology of trading is discussed in more detail in Chapter 9.

Trading CFDs

CFDs are the retail trading product of the future. I have spoken to many large-scale private traders who think CFDs are a bonanza. I believe the ranks of full-time CFD traders will swell as the benefits catch on. Trading hasn't become any easier with the introduction of CFDs, but it has certainly become cheaper and simpler. The ability to take very small positions with no or low commission and a small amount of capital is the ultimate environment to learn and improve your trading strategy.

Start small, dream big.

chapter 2

FREQUENTLY ASKED QUESTIONS

What is a CFD?

A contract for difference, or 'CFD', is a contract between you and your CFD provider to settle the difference in cash between the price at which you buy the CFD and the price at which you sell.

The price of a share CFD mirrors the underlying share price. For example if the price of Telstra is quoted on the exchange at $4.34–$4.35 then the CFD on Telstra will have the same quote. If the price of Telstra moves up in the underlying market then so does the CFD. For most markets there is no difference between the CFD prices and the underlying share prices in the physical market.

Therefore, instead of buying or selling physical shares, the CFD holder gets access to the performance—or price movements of a share—without ever having to take delivery of the actual shares.

Where did CFD trading originate?

CFDs originated in the global institutional and interbank market in the 1980s. In this environment, they are known as equity swaps and are a common way for banks and institutions to hedge share positions. CFD trading has been available to private traders since 1999 when a UK broker first offered the service to retail investors.

Since then, the popularity of CFDs has skyrocketed. Initial interest grew on the back of the stock market boom of the late 1990s when UK investors sought to avoid stamp duty. In the last few years CFDs have become even more popular as investors take advantage of the ability to take short positions or make money from a falling market. The UK market now has numerous players, including a number of traditional stockbrokers who have realised the enormous popularity of this instrument and added CFD trading to their product range.

The Financial Services Reform Act (FSRA) came into effect in Australia on 11 March 2002. It opened the market for international firms to offer products previously unseen in Australia. There are currently only a few CFD providers in Australia. More stockbrokers and specialist CFD providers are likely to offer this service as the popularity of CFDs grows.

A CFD is collateral financed; what does this mean?

This means that you must put down a deposit in order to secure the trade. This deposit is not a down-payment in order to pay for the balance of the trade. Instead, it is a 'margin' held by your provider as protection against any possible losses.

A CFD trades on margin. The margin is the security needed by your CFD provider enabling you to trade, commonly 5, 10 or 20 per cent for share trades and less for sector trades and indices.

17

How does a CFD work?

You believe Telstra will rise in price and decide to buy, or go long, 1,000 Telstra CFDs at the market price $4.35. The value of this position is $4,350. You are required to have 5 per cent margin to secure the trade which is calculated as:

$$\$4,350 \times 5\% = \$217.50$$

You hold the position open overnight and, because you are long, you will incur a financing charge. The rate at which you are charged finance is determined by your CFD provider. Usually, this rate is based on the official cash rate in the underlying market plus a small margin. It is similar to paying interest on the value of your house. If you have a mortgage each month you will be paying interest to the bank to service your debt. Your mortgage rate is determined by reference to the tenor of your loan (say, 25 years), the interest rate that corresponds to that tenor, plus a margin for the bank.

What costs are involved?

Brokerage rates vary between CFD providers. For share CFDs they range from a minimum of $10 per side up to 0.4 per cent of the underlying value of the trade. Sector and index trades are generally commission free. If you are long or have bought a CFD position and hold it overnight, you will pay a finance charge on the value of your position. If you are short a CFD overnight you may receive interest on the value of your position, depending on the prevailing interest rates in the underlying market.

You will pay or receive interest on 100 per cent of the value of the underlying position. There are no deductions for the 5 per cent you have used as the initial margin to secure the trade. This is because that 5 per cent is not a down-payment on the rest of the value of the position. Rather, it is a security held by your provider against any possible losses incurred on the position.

Why do financing costs exist?

Financing costs and benefits are the debits and credits made to your account on a daily basis, reflecting the interest expense of holding a long position or the benefit of holding a short position overnight.

A long position is the equivalent of borrowing money on an asset. Interest is charged on the value of the asset that you have borrowed on a daily basis at the market rate (which fluctuates) plus a margin for the facilitator.

The reverse is true for a short position. This simulates the situation you would be in if you had lent money. Every day you may receive interest on the total value of your position at the market rate, less a margin for the facilitator.

Financing costs and benefits apply to CFDs because you are dealing on margin and not paying the full value of your trade in order to secure the transaction. That means you pay or receive interest on the full 100 per cent value of your position rather than just the net of margin amount.

Financing costs apply because if your provider was to directly hedge your deal in the underlying market they would have to use their capital to fund 100 per cent of the position. Dealing on margin is the equivalent of the CFD provider lending you the money to fund your deal.

When a CFD trader goes short, it is the equivalent of lending the CFD provider the position which they can then use to offset other opposite positions. Because the CFD provider is using the full value of the position, they pay interest on the full value of the position to the client and this acts as a type of incentive to provide these trades to the provider. It is also like lending stock and receiving a return for the stock you have lent. In many instances, for a market maker to accumulate offsetting positions from its clients, rather than enter the underlying physical market to hedge, they are happy to provide a yield to clients to short a position. In this way CFDs mirror the underlying market they represent.

Financing costs also provide the market maker an opportunity to make money from financing your deal. This is why it is important you compare them. Just as a mortgage lender adds a 'haircut' to the interest rate that it is prepared to lend money at, so does your CFD provider. This is one avenue available to them to make money.

The size of the haircut can make CFDs look more attractive in terms of breakeven costs, especially in comparison to leveraged equity portfolios, or balanced long/short portfolios. For example, the rate of interest that you pay has a direct impact on your breakeven price. For a long position it will be detrimental and for a short position it will be incremental.

If you were to buy 1,000 TLS share CFDs at $4.00 and hold the position for three days you would incur a financing charge of $2.20. This means that to sell your position at breakeven you must sell at $4.002 or better. Each day you hold the long position your breakeven price will increase, albeit at very small increments.

For a short position the benefits in terms of breakeven are ongoing for as long as you have your position open. Each day you receive financing benefits your breakeven share price will reduce. It is possible that, if the market did not move and you received finance for long enough, you could be in a profitable trade by virtue of just holding the position. This is a consideration, but it should not be a motivation to trade given that the financing costs and benefits are small compared to market movements and their relative velocity.

How do you calculate the finance cost?

Let's say the official cash rate in Australia (set by the Reserve Bank of Australia) is 4.75 per cent (per annum) and the margin—the haircut—applied by your CFD provider is 1.0 per cent. Therefore, you would pay interest at an annual rate of 4.75 per cent plus 1.0 per cent, which is a total of 5.75 per cent on the value of your open position on a daily basis. In the earlier example of TLS shares, the financing cost is calculated as:

$$(\$4{,}350 \times 5.75\%) / 365 = 68.53¢ \text{ per day}$$

How do you calculate the profit or loss?

Let's say you close the TLS position after three days at a price of $4.48. Your profit is calculated as the difference in the price you entered and exited the trade, multiplied by the size of your position:

$$13¢ \times 1{,}000 = \$130.00$$

Financing costs are recalculated and deducted from your account on a daily basis. Three days of financing cost at around 69¢ per day gives net proceeds of:

$$\$130 - (69¢ \times 3) = \$127.93 \text{ net profit}$$

Hence, you have made a profit of around $127.93 from an initial investment of $217.50. This is a return on your initial investment of 58 per cent. The relatively high return is a reflection of the small capital outlay required to secure the trade. This is the advantage of trading with leverage—it magnifies returns.

But, be warned, leverage means that losses are also magnified. If Telstra had fallen 13¢ in three days the net proceeds would be calculated as:

$$-\$130 - \$2.07 = \$132.07 \text{ net loss}$$

Do I receive dividends, stock splits or other shareholder benefits?

Yes. Corporate actions such as dividends, rights issues and stock splits are emulated in the CFD market with either cash adjustments, CFDs on rights or splitting CFD positions to mirror the underlying market. However, the CFD holder does not have voting rights. The benefits are credited to traders with long CFD positions and deducted on short positions.

Do dividend payments include tax?

A CFD cannot take into account any client's individual tax positions. This is why, in Australia, tax adjustments such as franking or imputation credits do not apply to CFDs.

Is the CFD market regulated?

CFDs are regulated by the Australian Securities and Investments Commission (ASIC) as off-exchange OTC (over-the-counter) equity derivatives. Being derivative instruments in their own right means there are no restrictions on shorting (i.e. selling in anticipation of a fall in prices) or which stocks can be represented as a CFD.

How do CFDs compare with futures?

Both are traded on margin, requiring an initial margin and a variation margin to cover price movements against you. The initial margin is treated as a security against loss for both instruments, not a down-payment.

However, futures contracts are traded on an exchange (typically in Australia on the Sydney Futures Exchange, or SFE), cleared through an official clearing house and transacted for you by your broker. In contrast, CFDs are transacted with either a broker or market maker, but the counter-party to your trade is always the CFD provider rather than another trader.

The integrity of a futures contract is guaranteed by a clearing house who assures the settlement of your contract. Futures contracts may be cash-settled or, in the case of commodity futures, 'held till delivery'. When a futures contract is held until delivery, the seller of the contract must deliver to the buyer the goods on which the contract is based. For example, the seller of an oil contract would be expected to deliver barrels of oil equal to the contract value of the position.

Most financial futures contracts are cash settled. The Share Price Index (SPI) futures contract is an example of a cash-settled contract. Such a futures contract is, in effect, a contract for difference, because the difference in the prices at which you entered and exited the trade is settled in cash and guaranteed by the clearing house.

Unlike futures, CFDs are traded off-exchange. The guarantor of your contract is your CFD provider. Because CFDs are not limited to any one single exchange, often your CFD provider— if they are a market maker—is able to provide access to many different global markets. Indeed, if your provider of CFDs is a market maker, your transactions costs as a client can be eliminated, as there is no need to clear the trade through an exchange. Therefore, many providers can offer you numerous international markets and allow you to trade via one currency account. This is not possible when dealing in exchange-traded products with your broker.

The other major difference is in the way a contract is specified and priced. Futures contracts are all standardised in order to facilitate liquidity. CFDs are also standardised, but in values or units of one. For example, the standard tick value of an SPI futures contract is $25 per point, whereas the standard tick value of the equivalent CFD is totally flexible and can be as little as $1 per point. This means you can tailor your exposure.

How do index CFD prices compare to index futures spreads?

CFD prices are based on the indices with reference to the underlying futures market. CFD prices can be as narrow as—or even narrower than—the futures market, depending on how keenly priced your CFD provider is. This will often be a function of the amount of business they are seeing as a market maker. For example, CMC Group quote the US30 Index price at 5 points wide, Dow futures often trade at 8 points wide, and some CFD providers quote a spread up to 14 points wide.

There is an adjustment to your account each day when your trade is rolled over. This rollover reflects the fair value of your position and is made up of both interest and dividends. With a futures contract this cost, or benefit, is already capitalised into the price that you are dealing at. Typically, the bid will be higher for a futures contract where there are no dividends expected until maturity. Hence, on a futures contract you will be buying at a higher price, whereas on a CFD you pay a lower price but also pay daily finance charges. Over time the higher futures price will converge to equal the sum of the lower CFD price adding in the financing costs. The same is true in reverse for a short position.

What is fair value?

In basic terms fair value is the difference between the futures price and the cash price of an index. For example, SPI futures may be trading at 2965 and the S&P/ASX 200 level is 2950. The fair value is 15 points (not including spread basis).

When commentators talk about the futures trading at a 'discount' or 'premium' to the cash market this can be explained by fair value.

How is fair value calculated?

In the above example, the futures price is at a premium to the cash price. Fair value is a reflection of the yield curve and dividend. Using the above example, let's say the time to expiry was 68 days away and today the cash price is 2950. With interest rates at the time of writing at 4.75 per cent, if we were to express this cash price in terms of the future date we would come up with 2976.11. First establish the interest component:

$$2950 \times 4.75\% \times 68/365 = 26.11$$

Then add this component to the futures price:

$$2950 + 26.11 = 2976.11$$

Taking into account current interest rates we would calculate the value of the futures contract at expiry to be 2976.11. However, looking back to our example, the current futures price is 2965. Why the difference? This is because the calculation performed above does not take into account the expectations over that 68-day period. For instance, from now until expiry 12 stocks in the S&P/ASX 200 plan to pay dividends. The amount of the forecast dividend is adjusted for the weight of the stock within the index and then converted into a point value. This amount of index points is subtracted from the interest premium we calculate before. Therefore the new equation is:

$$\text{Fair Value} = \text{Interest Premium} + \text{Expected Dividends}$$
$$FV = 26.11 - 11$$
$$FV = 15.11$$

Therefore the S&P/ASX 200 is calculated as the futures price of 2965 − 15 = 2950, which is usually in line with the cash price of the underlying index.

Each day the expiry date draws closer, the fair value usually decreases until the price of the futures contract and the cash market converge at expiry. On the Wednesday before the Thursday expiry the fair value might be 16 and on Thursday it might be 15. This 1 point difference represents the amount of your index CFD rollover. Therefore, if you were long the S&P/ASX 200 at 2950 on Wednesday, on Thursday you would be long at 2952. A positive yield curve that outweighs the effects of dividend expectations will translate to a cost to go long and a benefit to go short on the rollover. In reality there is very little difference. The rollover component in a CFD is capitalised into a futures price. On a practical level that means instead of paying or receiving a rollover each day, you simply buy at a higher or sell at a lower futures price.

How does the CFD provider calculate the price of the index CFD?

This is how the CFD index pricing process works:

↳ You buy the Aussie 200 CFD at 2950. You pay 1 point rollover after day one, which means on day two you can now sell the CFD at 2950.

↳ You buy the SPI index future at 2965. There is no rollover to pay after day one; you can sell the SPI at 2964 on the following day.

↳ The net effect is that holding the position overnight costs one index point regardless of the whether you trade a futures contract or an index CFD.

The advantage of trading index CFDs is the ability to trade a price that looks similar to the underlying index and does not involve a broker or brokerage costs.

Do CFDs have expiry dates like futures contracts?

No. CFDs are priced as a daily contract, whereas futures contracts expire on a certain date in the future. Thus, futures contracts have a cost of carry inbuilt into the price that you are buying or selling at on any particular day. The cost of carry includes the interest rate consideration on the value of the contract until the expiry date, less the expected dividends over that period. CFDs make that adjustment to the value of your contract on a daily basis. This is most obvious when comparing single stock futures to CFDs.

Why would I trade an equity CFD instead of a single stock futures contract?

Single stock futures on a variety of exchanges around the world have been hampered by liquidity constraints. The nature of exchange-traded products means a tradeable market is not created until there are enough interested participants. This lack of liquidity is reflected in the spreads on single stock futures that tend to be wide, and lack of open interest. The CFD market is driven by the market makers and is therefore not contingent on client participation for liquidity.

What is the difference between a market maker and a broker?

When you enter a CFD with a market maker they are the counter-party to your trade. Most CFD providers are market makers. However, some are only brokers, which means they will facilitate the transaction between yourself and another party—usually the CFD market maker.

How do CFDs compare with options?

There are two similarities between options and CFDS. The first is they both provide leverage to the trader. Secondly, both instruments allow the user to participate in the downside of falling markets by taking a short position. This is where the similarities end.

Buying an option involves the outlay of a premium to buy the right, but not the obligation, to buy or sell an underlying asset at a predetermined price. A call option is the right to buy shares at a predetermined price some time in the future, irrespective of where the market is. This can give the option buyer control over more shares than they could otherwise physically afford in the market for the same outlay.

To participate in downside movement you can buy a put option or sell a call—allowing you to collect premium and profit provided the price does not settle above your strike price.

Option pricing involves several elements: prevailing interest rates, dividend expectations, the current price of the share, its volatility over time and the time to expiry of the option. This complexity can often lead to a lack of transparency in pricing and a lack of liquidity in this type of derivative.

CFDs more closely resemble the price of the underlying market. This means determining the value on your CFD position is simply a matter of looking at the underlying share price, which is more widely available via a variety of media.

Because a CFD mirrors the price of the underlying share, you, as a client, have an independent pricing mechanism from your market maker. With an option, because the market determinants can vary, so can the price of the option, leaving you at the mercy of the skew of an individual market maker's book.

Here is an example of the pricing implications of buying a put option on News Corporation (NCP):

↳ The share price of NCP is currently $10.98 and the option's price is 36¢–38¢.

↳   Let's say you buy an NCP put option over 1,000 shares with a strike of 10.50 and an expiry of one month at 38¢. The price is expressed as the cost per share, so in this example the actual outlay is 1,000 × 38¢ = AUD$380.

The first confusing aspect of options trading is the price. The quote of 36¢–38¢ does not directly reflect the price of the underlying instrument. Also, the option's price is 2¢ wide. This is 5.5 per cent of the total option price compared to the CFD spread which is 2¢ or 1.8 per cent of the value of the NCP CFD. Clearly the option spread is wider and therefore going to require a much more dramatic move in order to breakeven.

How do CFDs compare with warrants?

Warrants can be viewed as long-dated options issued by a market maker. Few options providers allow you go short on warrants, but this does not mean your access to the downside is totally limited, as you can still buy a put. The problem for many traders using warrants is the price. Often premiums are expensive and the pricing unpredictable.

If you bought a Citibank warrant you are obliged to sell that warrant back to Citibank as it is not fungible with any other option provider's instruments.

How do CFDs compare with shares?

In many ways, dealing in traditional shares is very similar to dealing in CFDs. The price of the underlying market and the CFD will be the same. However, CFDs offer you a range of benefits and facilities that traditional share trading cannot. These features include the ability to go short, to trade on margin, to sell on a down-tick, the advantage of no commissions, no stamp duty or GST, access to many different denominated stocks in the one currency, the ability to trade world markets from one account, and the ability to trade indices and sectors.

What is the difference between spread betting and CFDs?

While the products may appear similar at first there are some key differences that can have a significant impact on your bottom line. Most spread betters don't charge commission, but spread betting is usually more costly than CFD trading.

CFDs offer the same spread as the underlying market. Financial spread betting in Australia is commission-free but there is an added hidden expense; the price you bet at is wider than the underlying market. The spread is widened by adding around 1 per cent of the value of the underlying to the current bid and offer.

What is the difference in cost of buying physical shares, buying CFDs and placing a spread bet?

Let's say Telstra is quoted at $4.93 (bid), $4.94 (ask) on the ASX. The CFD price at the same quote is $4.93–$4.94. The spread bet price is $4.90–$4.96. Therefore the price to buy Telstra for each of the three instruments is:

- ↳ Telstra shares at $4.94
- ↳ Telstra CFDs at $4.94
- ↳ Up-bet on Telstra at $4.96.

For a position of 10,000 shares you would pay your stock broker commission of around $50. At CMC Group, commission is charged at a rate of $10 per side for the first $10,000 and 0.1 per cent for positions in excess of $10,000 in value. That means your Telstra positions would attract commission of $49.40. To spread bet the equivalent of 10,000 shares is a bet of $100 per point. The offer price of $4.96 is 2¢ above, or $200 (i.e. $100 per point) worse than the current market price. This means that it costs you $150 more to take the same position with spread betting than CFDs.

Is it also more expensive to do a down-bet than to sell CFDs?

Yes, because the spread is widened with spread betting this also means it is effectively more costly to do a down-bet than to short CFDs.

Is there an expiry date for the spread bet or the CFD?

With a CFD you can leave the position open indefinitely. A spread bet position must be closed out after a day, week or quarter or, alternatively, arrangements for the bet to be rolled over must be made, which involves closing your old bet and opening a new one with a reduced spread. Different maturity dates on the spread bet mean each date will have a different and usually wider spread. The difference in prices takes into account the interest on the position and any forecast dividends. CFDs simply mirror the underlying market price on a day-by-day basis and move the same way as the underlying market.

Is the margin requirement different for spread betting compared to CFDs?

Spread betting in Australia usually requires a 10 per cent margin, which effectively means 10 times leverage on Australian stocks. Therefore, if you had $10,000 in your account you could have an up-bet for the equivalent of $100,000 worth of stock. The margin requirement for CFDs is between 5 and 20 per cent with CMC Group. This means a deposit of $10,000 can give you access to $200,000 underlying value of stock.

Is my money safe?

You must check the means and processes by which your CFD provider safeguards your funds. Often they will employ various prudential requirements that go beyond those of the regulator in that market, but different circumstance will apply for different markets on a geographical basis.

In Australia, your money will be protected by Australian Securities and Investments Commission client money rules. Ask your CFD provider if your funds are also placed in a segregated funds account. If this is the case, in the event of insolvency your funds are placed in trust for you as beneficiary.

Segregated funds accounts prevent the CFD provider from using client funds in the course of operating its business. Further, these funds are reconciled regularly, in order to mirror the balance of all client's equity, given the profits and losses experienced across the pool of accounts. In this way, all client funds are kept securely together and independent of the firm you are dealing with. In the unlikely event that your CFD provider did become insolvent, your funds could not be utilised and are placed in trust for the client.

This is the same method employed by futures brokers across Australia. However, it is not an obligation of the CFD provider to provide segregated accounts, so if you are unsure as to the credit-worthiness of the firm that you are dealing with, this may be a consideration.

The reason some firms may not want to offer segregated funds accounts is because they represent a drain on the company's capital (i.e. it prevents them being able to use client funds at other brokers to hedge those client positions). That is usually the only reason. It is unlikely a CFD company will use its client funds in the course of their daily business—for instance, paying their electricity bills!

Are my CFD profits subject to tax?

CFDs are sometimes confused with spread betting, which has been described as tax free. CFDs are regarded by the Australian Securities and Investments Commission as a derivative instrument and are therefore subject to the same tax treatment as, say, futures trading. Therefore, it is likely you will be obliged to pay tax according to your personal tax profile. For more information seek advice from your accountant.

If CFD providers charge low or no commission, how do they make money?

CFD providers make money in a number of ways. Firstly they will net the buy and sell orders and take the difference. For instance the spread for Telstra of $4.00–$4.01 would mean clients buy from the CFD provider at a price of $4.01 and the provider gives the CFD seller a price of $4.00. The difference is the middle is 1¢ per share and this is the profit to the CFD provider.

CFD providers will also make money by hedging their exposure in the institutional market. This means the CFD provider can deal at narrower spreads and, therefore, make the difference between the spread of the prices on offer to clients versus the spread enjoyed as a trader in the wholesale market.

Thirdly, the CFD provider makes money from the differential between the interest paid on short positions and the interest charged on long positions.

chapter 3

ADVANTAGES OF CFDs

NARROW SPREADS

CFD prices mirror those of the underlying market. This means CFDs give you access to the underlying market liquidity, plus the liquidity offered by the CFD provider itself. This is an important consideration when assessing the width of the spread you will be dealing on and how the spread is calculated. A lack of liquidity in a market leads to wide spreads and results in a market becoming less attractive to trade.

Liquidity is Important

A lack of liquidity has plagued the market in single stock futures, options and warrants. Up until the introduction of CFDs, local investors wanting access to leveraged products were limited to these instruments. With futures there are only few participants making prices, and with options and warrants even fewer. Warrant providers can be even less competitive since you must enter and exit the trade with the same provider.

A lack of depth and liquidity in these markets has resulted in non-competitive pricing and poor returns for private investors.

CFDs Reflect Liquidity of the Underlying Market

There are thousands of participants in the stock market at any point in time. The collective effect of actual business and underlying demand creates competitive pricing, which means narrow spreads. CFDs are priced using the underlying sharemarket and are therefore able to use the liquidity of that market, while combining the benefits of leverage and long and short trading that the derivatives markets provide. This is an extremely powerful formula and has contributed to the growth in popularity of CFDs.

The Cost Impact of Spreads

Narrow spreads help the trader by reducing the cost of transacting and increasing the odds in the trader's favour. Excluding commissions and taxes the spread is usually the most expensive part of any trade. The cost of the spread can be easily calculated by taking the number of shares you are trading and dividing by 100. You are actually dividing by the number of cents in the dollar. For example, say the price of Telstra is $4.04–$4.05 and you wish to buy 1,000 share CFDs. You will be able to buy them at $4.05. The value of this trade is $4,050. If you wanted to immediately sell them again, you would be selling at $4.04, and the value of this trade would be $4,040. The difference is $10 which is the cost of the spread. Quickly and easily this can be calculated as 1,000 shares divided by 100¢, which equals $10.

You can apply this rule to every market that is dealt in denominations of 100 (for example, dollars and cents in the US, euros and cents in most of Europe, francs and centimes in Switzerland, and pounds and pence in the UK).

Spreads Impact Profitability

Trading is a matter of balancing the odds in your favour as much as possible. If you trade through a traditional broker, it is most likely that you are only trading the long side or buying shares. Most people believe they have a 50/50 chance that the security they are trading can move in their favour. In reality this situation is like sitting a test where the pass mark is 75 per cent but you answer only 75 out of 100 of the questions in the test. To achieve this result you will have to get 100 per cent of the questions right that you answer. It is more difficult because you have no flexibility to get any questions wrong. You need to answer all the questions in order to maximize your odds of getting that result. The same principle applies to CFDs. Rather than just trying to find profitable long trades in the market, you can also look for downside opportunities.

There are three directions that can take place in a market—it can move up, down, or sideways and do nothing. If you use a traditional broker and only buy shares, you are only exposing yourself to one of three possible outcomes. When trading CFDs you can go long and you can go short (see page 44). You can even receive interest when the market is going sideways on a short position. You have all possible outcomes covered. Having all this flexibility in one product increases your odds of success in the market.

NO COMMISSIONS AND LOW TRANSACTION COSTS

Working as a futures broker, I saw many day-trading systems that failed. These systems were profitable in a test environment, but when they were traded in the real world, the results were either very low profits or losses. Often it was the brokerage costs that were the deciding factor. It is common for a day-trading system to show a profit when brokerage is taken out of the equation. Commission is a crucial element in your trading system and CFDs open new trading opportunities because they have reduced or eliminated this overhead.

Commissions and Breakeven Costs

High commission charges increase your breakeven costs. Let's take a typical example with a broker. Assume you buy 1,000 TLS shares at $4.05, and pay $20 commission and a further 10 per cent GST on the trade. This can be seen in Figure 3.1 (opposite) from the CMC Group website, where you can compare a traditional share trade with a CFD trade. Transaction costs will increase your breakeven cost to $4.0940 on the trade. This is an increase of close to 4.5¢ or over 1 per cent. Not only would you have to cross the spread, you would also have to make a gross profit to pay transaction costs. In this way transaction costs place the odds against you.

The Effect of Financing on Breakeven

Using a CFD, the breakeven increases by the amount of the financing costs each day. You can see in Figure 3.1, the breakeven has increased by 0.0007 to $4.0507. This is an almost negligible difference to the odds of success. Using a comparison screen such as that opposite from the dealforfree.com website, the differences in breakeven become obvious.

You should compare both spread size and transaction costs at the same time. There is no point dealing on wide spreads and paying low commission, or paying excessive commissions to deal on market prices. The optimal outcome for your bottom line is to deal at a price that mirrors the underlying market with low commission.

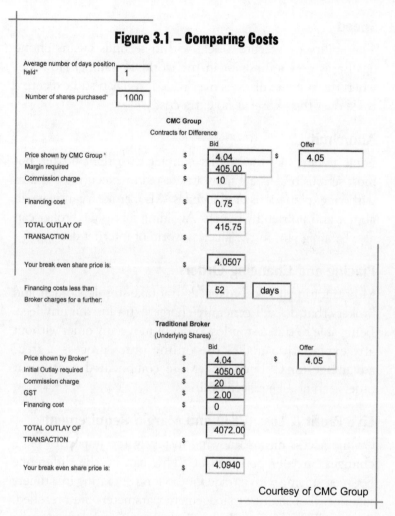

Figure 3.1 – Comparing Costs

Average number of days position held* [1]

Number of shares purchased* [1000]

CMC Group
Contracts for Difference

		Bid		Offer
Price shown by CMC Group *	$	4.04	$	4.05
Margin required	$	405.00		
Commission charge	$	10		
Financing cost	$	0.75		
TOTAL OUTLAY OF TRANSACTION	$	415.75		
Your break even share price is:	$	4.0507		
Financing costs less than Broker charges for a further:		52	days	

Traditional Broker
(Underlying Shares)

		Bid		Offer
Price shown by Broker*	$	4.04	$	4.05
Initial Outlay required	$	4050.00		
Commission charge	$	20		
GST	$	2.00		
Financing cost	$	0		
TOTAL OUTLAY OF TRANSACTION	$	4072.00		
Your break even share price is:	$	4.0940		

Courtesy of CMC Group

ONLINE ACCESS

Local traders who are using overseas CFD providers that have established branches here in Australia will benefit from the company's evolution in a competitive and sophisticated market. The online facilities are now better than you will find from most online stockbrokers.

Speed

The ability to execute a deal within seconds means phone dealing is now a dinosaur in the world of trading. However, when the system fails or is overloaded, you can still execute a trade over the phone at no extra cost.

Anonymity

Some traders like the regular contact with their broker, but most serious traders are more interested in executing the deal without explanations or platitudes. Also, brokers can seem an abrupt and unfriendly bunch. Avoiding a brusque broker can also be a big plus in the faceless world of internet dealing.

Placing and Changing Orders

Most traditional stockbrokers do not take stop-loss orders and brokers that do will generally charge extra for the privilege. Being able to trail a stop-loss order or move any order without any explanation makes the online order process a great advantage for CFD traders. More complicated contingent orders can also be placed online.

Live Profit & Loss (P&L) and Margin Requirement

Online access means knowing instantly the impact of price changes on your bottom line. This can be the difference between staying with a trade for too long or exiting in a timely manner when money management parameters are breached. A good CFD provider will also display your margin requirement online. This means you know at any time how much funds are at your disposal.

Live Charting

The charting package offered by most CFD providers will not be sophisticated. However, free intraday charts, even if they don't have all the bells and whistles, are a great advantage for small private traders.

24-Hour Access

Being able to participate in a market anywhere in the world means CFD trading is a 24-hour trading facility. A single currency account gives you access to global stocks and indices without paying commission even for foreign market transactions.

TRANSPARENT PRICING

One of the biggest attractions of CFD trading is the way in which the price of a CFD trades in tandem with the price of the underlying. Because the prices of the CFDs mirror the underlying market they are one of the most transparently priced derivative tools available to private clients.

Pricing Mirrors Physical

Making money from trading is challenging enough without the prices you execute your trades being based on sophisticated concepts that need special evaluation and extra analysis. Option and warrant pricing is a good example of this. The option premium is based on the price of the underlying but also includes other factors such as time to expiry, volatility and even the current exposure of the option or warrant market maker. Small traders must not only meet the challenge of picking the right direction, but also the sophistication of the pricing model. When factors not directly priced into the value of the underlying security can impact the price in a way that is not straightforward, the derivative instrument can be intimidating for the private trader and place him or her at a distinct disadvantage.

Market Depth

Most CFD providers offer spreads on CFDs that reflect the underlying exchange. However sometimes when you attempt to place an order you may find the price is requoted and is wider. If your order is larger than the current bid and offer shown by the underlying exchange then the CFD provider will show a price to accommodate your volume. CFD traders can use the market depth information provided by the underlying stock exchange to determine the impact of their orders on the CFD market. This is because the CFD provider will move the price according to the market depth on the underlying exchange. An order to buy at the offer price quoted on the ASX is usually only valid for the amount of shares on offer according to the ASX system. Market depth reveals orders underlying the current bid and offer and this forms the basis of the spread when a client is trying to deal at a volume that is larger than the current spread.

For example the quote on the ASX for Leighton Holdings Limited (LEI) is $9.30–$9.31 (at the time of writing). The market depth data shown in Figure 3.2 (opposite) reveals the order sizes. Let's say you wished to buy 10,000 CFDs on LEI. However, there are only 121 shares on offer for LEI at the current offer of $9.31. The next offer prices are $9.32 for 19 shares, $9.33 for 7,713 shares and $9.39 with 10,000 shares available. This means if you were to buy 10,000 physical shares of LEI at market you would be quoted an average price based on the market depth. This would mean you obtained:

- ↳   122 shares at $9.31
- ↳   19 at $9.32
- ↳   7,713 at $9.33
- ↳   2,146 at $9.39.

Figure 3.2 – Market Depth

LEI - Leighton Holdings Limited

Last traded at:
16-Apr-2003 11:34:56 AM

Last	Movement		Bid	Ask	Open	High	Low	Trades	Volume
9.310	⬆ 0.010	0.11 %	9.300	9.310	9.370	9.370	9.300	59	69,151

	Buyers				Sellers		
Number	Quantity	Price		Price	Quantity		Number
6	30,457	9.300	1	9.310	122		1
1	1,000	9.290	2	9.320	19		1
2	2,640	9.270	3	9.330	7,713		3
1	1,000	9.260	4	9.390	10,706		1
4	14,385	9.250	5	9.400	14,500		4
1	2,100	9.240	6	9.430	1,000		1
1	300	9.230	7	9.440	2,100		1
1	150	9.220	8	9.450	53,229		3
8	6,536	9.200	9	9.460	2,000		1
1	1,000	9.170	10	9.470	6,990		2
4	2,428	9.160	11	9.480	2,000		1
2	1,300	9.150	12	9.490	6,590		3
1	1,500	9.140	13	9.500	2,883		5
1	1,090	9.130	14	9.510	300		1
3	2,550	9.120	15	9.550	12,733		4
10	12,715	9.100	16	9.590	750		1
2	2,750	9.090	17	9.600	8,100		5
2	2,180	9.080	18	9.620	5,000		1
2	2,500	9.070	19	9.650	10,000		1
7	7,040	9.050	20	9.660	2,222		2

Courtesy of InvestorWeb Research (www.investorweb.com.au)

To get the average price, multiply each offer price by the number of shares:

122	×	9.31	=	1,135.82
19	×	9.32	=	177.08
7,713	×	9.33	=	71,962.29
2,146	×	9.39	=	20,150.94

Now, add the total of the above calculation and divide by 10,000:

$$\frac{93{,}426.1}{10{,}000}$$

This equals 9.34. Thus, if you wanted to buy 10,000 of LEI, your CFD provider would offer you a price of $9.34. This would represent a 3¢ difference from the current ASX offer price, but if you were to place the same market order in the physical market, the actual fill price would be the same.

LEVERAGE

Leverage can be a double-edged sword. But, in the hands of a disciplined trader it provides cheap access to potentially huge profits.

Margin Levels

Most CFD providers will require a margin deposit of around 5 per cent to 10 per cent of the underlying value of the position. This covers your account for a move in price against the position and is, therefore, returned to you when the position is closed out at a profit. If your position is closed out at a loss, the money will be netted against the margin amount.

Capital Preservation

The concept of leverage means you can take a relatively small proportion of your available investment capital to trade CFDs. This means the majority of your capital can stay in long-term investments.

GOING SHORT

Making money from a fall in prices is known as going short. Some traditional sharebrokers allow clients to go short.

However, the shorting facility with a stockbroker is more complicated and costly than selling short a CFD.

Enter on a Down-Tick

When going short with a stockbroker you can only open a short position on an up-tick. That means the last traded price must have been made on the offer price of a buy. This would mean buying on a potential bounce in a downtrend, which flouts the rule of trading with the trend. This also means that an investor cannot participate in a potentially large sell-off in a share unless there is an up-tick in this process and they are lucky enough to 'get set' or be executed. This prevents traders from joining in some of the dramatic downtrends that can start as soon as the session opens for a stock. With a CFD there is no restriction on when you open a position. If there are enough bids on the underlying market to fill your sell order, you can go short.

No Other Special Requirements

Shorting facilities are usually only offered by full-service brokers and, as a result, the commission charges will be higher than standard brokering costs. This means paying around $75 to open a short position. With CFDs, a short position has lower commission or is commission-free in the case of an index or sector CFD. The margin requirements for shorting with a traditional stockbroker are usually 20 per cent of the underlying value of the position. With CFDs, there is no difference between going long and going short and for a share CFD the margin requirement is usually between 5 and 20 per cent.

Receive Interest

Going short with CFDs also involves the added bonus of receiving interest on the notional value of your position. The interest paid is usually based on the official cash rate of the underlying market less a percentage nominated by the CFD provider. This haircut is usually around 1.0 per cent to 1.5 per cent. The interest amount is recalculated each day, based on the closing price of the underlying, and paid into your account on a daily basis.

GLOBAL MARKET ACCESS WITH NO TAXES

Buying and selling shares on overseas markets is as simple as investing on the local market when you trade CFDs. From one account you can short sell Microsoft CFDs or buy British Telecom CFDs, all commission- and tax-free. The tax-free factor is important if you intend to trade offshore share CFDs. In the UK investors are charged stamp duty when they trade physical shares. However, CFDs are not subject to stamp duty and this can represent a significant saving.

chapter 4

GETTING STARTED

QUESTIONS TO ASK YOUR CFD PROVIDER

The CFD market, especially in Australia, is relatively new for retail traders. Despite many traders having years of derivative trading experience, a lot of new CFD traders have a very rudimentary understanding of the product before they sign up with a provider. Therefore, there are some important questions that can affect your bottom line, which every potential client should ask.

What spread do you charge?

While brokerage is an obvious charge, the spread can also add expense to the trading process. The wider the spread, the more it will cost you to transact a trade. Ideally the spread should imitate the spread quoted on the exchange on which the CFD is based. If it is wider than the exchange spread, then the CFD provider has built a transaction cost into the prices. It is not common practise for CFD providers to charge a spread on

CFDs, however spread betting, which is commonly and mistakenly compared to CFDs, is characterised by wide spreads.

For example, let's say the stock exchange is quoting stock XYZ at $10.00 to buy and $10.02 to sell.

CFD Provider No.1 quotes the same rate. CFD/spread bet provider No.2 quotes a bid price of $9.95 and an offer price of $10.07. This effectively means for every share CFD you buy, you will pay an extra 5¢ per share. On a position of 1,000 shares this would add up to an extra cost of $50 and on a 10,000 position that would be a $500 extra charge. This is where the CFD/spread bet provider will earn extra income from your business.

What are your commission rates?

Some CFD providers charge higher commission than others. The rates may vary from 0.1 per cent at CMC Group to as much as 0.4 per cent, based on the underlying value of the position. Often the CFD provider who charges commission will prescribe a minimum deal size. This means they can guarantee a certain level of commission per trade. In such cases, $40 may be the minimum brokerage payable.

For example, if you wished to buy $10,000 worth of share CFDs on stock XYZ: the CFD provider charges 0.4 per cent on the trade, which means it costs you:

$$10,000 \times 0.004 = \$40$$

Can I trade online?

Online trading is now extremely popular, and the preferred method of execution for many traders. A good online trading system should provide live prices, live charting, and news. Take advantage of any trial software offer to test for user-friendliness, charting and news features, the ability to leave orders, position keeping and live profit and loss update, as well as speed of execution. A 24-hour dealing platform should also be accompanied by an efficient 24-hour technical support desk. It is also worth asking your CFD provider how long the company has been offering its dealing platform to ensure it has proven reliability.

What are your financing rates?

These should be fixed to an official rate such as the overnight cash rate of the country in which the underlying stock exchange operates. For instance, in Australia the rate is generally set around the Reserve Bank of Australia overnight rate, with an additional 1 to 2 per cent for buying and subtracting the same amount for selling. This impacts the daily cost or benefit of holding a position and it is worthwhile comparing the borrowing and lending rates from your CFD provider.

How does a margin call work?

Before you start trading, it is important to understand the margin call process. A margin call will occur if the money in your account falls to a level below the prescribed rate for the combination of the positions in your account and the losses against it. This will help you avoid any awkward situations where you are unable to meet a margin call in a timely manner and the CFD provider is forced to close out your position. The margin call level will differ between CFD providers. Some CFD providers with online dealing platforms also have an automatic real-time margining system. This can keep you continually abreast of the impact of price development on your margin requirements.

SETTING UP YOUR ACCOUNT

Setting up your account can be a lengthy process. If you are keen to get trading it is important that you are aware of the time involved to complete paperwork, have it approved and allow funds to clear.

Application Forms

Apart from supplying personal details, the main objective of providing an application form is to assess the trading experience and financial suitability of a potential client for CFD trading. This is a prudential measure not only imposed by the regulators but by the CFD provider themselves. Often it will not be obvious on the application form, but certain questions are intended to satisfy the CFD provider's 'rule of thumb' before deeming you suitable to trade CFDs. The two most important criteria for the CFD provider are a minimum of six months relevant trading experience and a net asset value (excluding the value of your dwelling) to risk capital of 5:1.

Product Disclosure Statement

Regulators require full disclosure of the products and services offered by your CFD provider. In Australia this is required by ASIC for the benefit of both the company and the client. Dealing and pricing policies, client and company obligations, taxation considerations, dispute resolution procedures, client money rules, and material risks are all disclosed along with any fees and charges. This is the nitty gritty of running an account and not 'fine print' to be overlooked. Much of the time the only risks clients think about with regard to CFDs are the swings of the market. However, as much importance should be placed on the product itself.

Risk Capital

Do not trade with money you cannot afford to lose! We have all heard this before. If your CFD provider is a good one, there will be certain processes, procedures and filters behind the scenes that the company will employ to protect over exuberant clients from their own trading folly. It is not in your CFD provider's interests to take on an account of $100,000 from a client whose net worth is only $100,000. The more prudent ratio of 5:1 would mean a client with a net worth of $100,000 trades an account size of not more than $20,000.

Transferring Funds

Most CFD providers in Australia use the BPAY system. You can also deposit via a cheque, telegraphic transfer, and credit card. However, BPAY is the cheapest and fastest option available. It is important to realise that you will not be able to trade until you have cleared funds in your account. It is best to transfer funds to the CFD provider well before you intend to take your first trade.

MARGIN CALLS

Unlike share trading, where you are required to pay the entire value of your position upfront, CFD trading involves the payment of a margin. For most CFD providers this is in the range of 5 to 20 per cent of the total value of the underlying cost of the holding. This is essentially a deposit or insurance policy against a movement in the price of the underlying that would cause you to incur a loss.

If this movement against you reaches a certain level, it will cause you to receive a margin call. This means depositing more money into your account to cover the loss-making position. Margin calls are part and parcel of leveraged trading.

For example, if you were to buy 20,000 CFDs on Telstra at $4 with a 5 per cent margin your deposit would be calculated as:

$$20,000 \times \$4.00 \times 5\% = \$4,000$$

Each 1¢ move in the value of the shares would equal $200. If your account balance was $5,000 then a 5¢ movement in the value of the underlying share would trigger a margin call.

Taking a position that requires a large proportion of your deposit can be a common mistake with new CFD traders. Many traders find the opportunity to take a leveraged position a very attractive proposition. They will frequently maximise their positions to the point where there is very little money left in the account to cover a move against the position. The Telstra trade above is a good example. With only $1,000 left in the account to cover a move down in price, the share price would only have to decrease by a very small amount before the account holder would be on margin call.

If you open an account with a minimum deposit and then place an order that uses most of your capital, you are making it very difficult to maintain the position as it experiences day-to-day volatility. Very few trades stay in profit from the moment they are opened. Studying the historical volatility of the underlying share or index should alert the trader to the kind of swings that he or she needs to cater for.

A margin call can have a serious impact on the emotional aspect of your trading. As a broker, I saw many sound trades closed at a loss on a margin call. Frequently these trades then proceeded to go back into profit. Margin calls can make you think you have a flawed trading system when, in reality, your have either underfunded your account or taken a position that is too large.

The best CFD traders never allow themselves to be in a position of receiving a margin call. They adequately fund their accounts and never trade above the deposit requirement. A margin call is a sign that an investor is trading beyond his or her trading aptitude. The easy way to ensure you trade within your means and abilities is to place a stop-loss order. The stop-loss can take you out of a position before you are given a margin call. The size of your CFD trade should reflect the volatility of the underlying as well as the size of your account.

THE ALTERNATIVE TO PAPER TRADING

If you have ever paper traded then you might recall a scenario that goes something like this:

1   **Day one:** you identify an entry price and write this down in your trading diary.

2   **Day two:** the price goes against you and you think about recording an exit but you don't.

3   **Day three:** the position goes back in your favour and, since you haven't written down the exit, you congratulate yourself on keeping the position going.

4   **Day four:** the position then shows a big profit; you start calculating profits in you head and tell yourself you should record an exit for this trade, but for some reason you forget.

5   **Day five:** the big profit starts to evaporate and you record an exit at yesterday's windfall result.

On paper you're a great trader! Wrong.

The problem with paper trading is everyone makes money. It's easy to be a winner on paper, much easier than trading with real dollars and cents.

Opinion is divided on the value of paper trading, and many experts in the field recommend new traders take imaginary positions to test their strategies and become accustomed to the trading process. There is nothing wrong with back-testing a strategy or approach by observing historical price action, but if you want to know the results of real-time trading your system, there is no substitute for putting your own money on the line.

Successful trading is more to do with your metal approach than the actual trading system you use. In my experience as a broker I saw winning and losing trades every day. I witnessed countless methods that work, but the consistently profitable traders have the right psychological approach. Mental discipline can only be developed through risking actual money. Money is the great motivator, making you stick to your rules and avoid taking big risks.

The ideal way for new traders to learn about trading, or for experienced traders to test a new trading system, is a compromise between risking significant trading capital and paper trading. This would involve investing with smaller amounts of capital. The problem with trading a small amount of capital in the traditional manner is that the transaction costs remain high. The brokerage charges of buying and selling a small parcel of shares can annihilate profits and exacerbate losses.

This is where CFDs come into the story. One of the biggest advantages of CFDs, especially CFDs provided by market makers who charge low commission, is the ability to play the market with a small amount of money with low overheads.

Low-commission share CFD and commission-free index and sector CFD trading allows traders to test indicators or strategies, putting a relatively small amount of money at risk without paying commission. A trader can literally trade the equivalent of as little as one share.

I know of a successful hedge fund management team that recently started trading CFDs. While they became accustomed to trading this new product, they placed very small trades. Compared to the $100 million plus they have under management, these professional traders were placing orders that had a margin requirement around $100.

Opposite is a comparison of taking a small position in shares versus a small size CFD trade.

Scenario

News Corporation Limited (NCP) is a popular stock on the Australian sharemarket for day traders. For the novice, a parcel of 50 NCP shares would be an affordable lesson with enough money involved to include the psychological aspect of the trade. The costs and capital required to buy 50 shares of NCP on the ASX when the price is quoted at $10.50–$10.51 is:

Buy 50 NCP at $10.51
Cost of shares = $525.50
Commission cost $30 plus GST of 10% or $3

Total outlay $558.50

Compare the above scenario with buying a low-commission CFD:

Buy 50 NCP CFDs at $10.51
Margin cost is 5 per cent of $525.50 which equals $26.28
Commission cost $10

Total outlay $36.28

In a week NCP has gained 50¢ and you exit the position. Proceeds of physical share position:

50 x $11.01 = $550.50
Commission cost $30 plus GST of 10% or $3
Proceeds $517.50

Net result $41.00 loss

The CFD position is calculated as follows:

50 x ($11.01 – $10.51) = $25.00
Commission cost $10
Interest charge (RBA overnight rate of 4.75% plus 1.0%) = 8.3¢ per day for seven days

Net result $4.42 profit

Reduced capital outlay is another advantage of small size CFD trading. Even if an investor wanted to use a traditional share trading approach eventually, testing the waters with CFDs can involve a marginal investment of just 5 per cent of the underlying value of the shareholding. This means serious capital is not tied up in the testing or education process and can be earning you interest elsewhere.

Having the discipline to stick with your system is the most important aspect of your trading approach. The process of being consistently profitable involves believing absolutely in your system. When you are completely resolved on the success of your system, you don't stray from its parameters. Until you put money on the line, you cannot know exactly how it will fair in the real world. While you can study the results of a back-tested or a paper trading system and consciously acknowledge its success, your subconscious doesn't believe it is successful until the money is in your pocket. It is within your subconscious that the success or failure of a system lies because it is the subconscious thoughts that undermine your approach and sabotage your system. CFDs allow you to trade real positions and prove the profitability of your approach with minimum capital on the line and minimum cost.

One of the most common mistakes of undisciplined traders is having a winning run and then giving it all back in one or two careless trades. I have observed numerous occasions where a trader has a winning streak and then makes a series of big losses. It is often nothing to do with the system and simply a matter of overconfidence that leads them to scrap their discipline. Until you gain experience in trading real money you cannot understand this process or the importance of the psychological input on your success. Small size CFD trading will allow you to understand this process intimately. It will show you the importance of building triggers and alarms into your system to prevent the big losing trade that can devastate your trading capital.

Placing Orders

Your CFD provider offers a range of order types that can help you maximise profits, enable clever entry points and prudent exit levels. The volatile nature of financial markets means a trade can be missed or an opportunity lost if you don't place an order beforehand.

There are two great advantages for placing orders rather than trading at market. The first is the ability to participate in market moves without having to watch the price action. The second advantage is the ability for a disciplined trader to use a premeditated and systematic approach. This means placing orders based on a planned strategy rather than reacting to the noise of the market and making emotional trading decisions.

Market Order and Limit Order

Like traditional stockbrokers, your CFD provider will offer two kinds of orders: market orders and limit orders. A market order means you deal at the price being bid or offered by the market maker or exchange. A limit order means you want to sell at a price above the current price or buy at a level below. With a limit you will never pay more than the nominated buy price or receive less than the nominated sell price.

Example: Telstra is trading at $4.00 and you have a long position on Telstra at $3.75. You wish to exit if the price goes up to $4.30:

'Sell Telstra at $4.30 on limit.'

Stop-loss Order

Possibly the most common mistake of new CFD traders is to open a position and not place a stop-loss order. Using stops means you are automatically taken out of a position if the market moves against you. Losing money is an inescapable element of trading, but limiting potential losses via a stop-loss can cut a losing trade before it becomes a painful mistake. Using a stop-loss is a cornerstone of disciplined trading.

Example: Telstra is trading at $4.00. You previously bought or went long at $3.80 and want to limit your loss if Telstra starts to fall. If it falls to the price you entered you want to exit the position:

'Sell Telstra CFD at $3.80 on stop.'

Stop-entry Order

A stop order can also be used to open a position with a sector or index CFD. If your trading strategy is trend-following or a break-out system then an 'on stop' entry order will automatically open a position.

Example: The Aussie 200 index is trading at 3400 and looks likely to fall at a break of 3380. If this happens, you wish to have a short position. The following order will give you an open position:

'Sell Aussie 200 at 3380 on stop.'

Guaranteed Stop-Loss Order

Some CFD providers offer a guaranteed stop-loss order facility. This service usually has an extra cost attached but it means there is no slippage on your order. Slippage describes the difference between the price you receive and the stop-loss order level on your original order. It occurs because prices can gap, move suddenly, or experience very low volume. This can happen on unexpected news or when important trigger levels are breached. To create certainty in your trading price a guaranteed stop-loss means your exit never suffers slippage.

If Done

An 'if done' order is a combination of two orders and is ideal for traders who cannot watch the market but want to make sure they participate in a move in their favour and/or exit a move against them.

Example: Telstra is trading at $4.00 and you wish to buy if it gets down to $3.80 but exit if the market then continues lower to $3.60:

'Buy Telstra at $3.80 limit; if done, sell at $3.60 on stop.'

One Cancels Other

One cancels other orders are generally said as the acronym 'OCO' and are another means to enter or exit the market without having to watch the price action. An OCO order has a number of advantages. It can be used to trade a break-out range, where you wish to sell if the price falls or buy if the price rises. It can also be used to simultaneously place a stop-loss and a limit to take profit.

Example: Telstra is trading at $4.00 and you have previously bought, or have a long position, at $3.80. You wish to exit your position at a profit if the price goes up to $4.50, or if the market moves lower first and you wish to be stopped out at $3.75:

'Sell Telstra at $4.50 on limit OCO $3.75 on stop.'

Good Till Cancelled

Good till cancelled, also known as 'GTC', is an attachment to an order. Instead of reminding your CFD provider to renew an order on a daily basis, a GTC order is worked until it is either filled or cancelled by you. Some CFD providers may only work a GTC order for a limited period, but generally they are indefinite.

Example: If you are short Telstra at $4.00 and you wish to exit if it rallies to $4.20:

'Buy Telstra at $4.20 on stop GTC.'

Order Types and Online Trading

Not all CFD providers offer the full range of orders electronically. Orders will often need to be changed regularly and many traders prefer to do this anonymously. Trailing stop-loss orders, where the trigger level tracks the latest trading price, are particularly high maintenance. Leaving orders via the telephone can be laborious and prone to human error. Therefore having a CFD provider with an electronic trading platform with the full range of orders can be an important advantage.

chapter 5

SHORT-TERM
MARKET ANALYSIS

There are many profitable trading strategies that work for all types of financial instruments. CFDs do not require a special set of trading rules or indicators. If you have a share or index trading strategy that is profitable with traditional shares, then the same system can be applied to CFDs, with the only difference being the benefit of no brokerage.

Since CFDs were introduced to private clients they have gained a reputation as the short-term traders' product of choice. CFDs are attractive to short-term traders because of the obvious benefits of low margin requirements and no commission. But one of the biggest advantages to short-term traders is the ability to leave stop-loss orders. The old trading rule 'don't be wrong for long' is easily adopted when you use the order system provided by online CFD providers. A common mistake of undisciplined traders is to turn a short-term play into a long-term losing position. With a stop-loss order in place, that losing day trade can be forgotten and not carried forward overnight in a desperate attempt to turn it into a profit.

One point to remember: if your trading strategy does not include a stop-loss level, it's not a strategy, it's just a punt.

In an environment of falling stock markets, CFDs have soared in popularity. For the first time small traders can short the market with the same ease as going long. There are no extra fees or collateral needed to short a CFD.

The trading approach I will go on to detail is not the 'Holy Grail' of CFD trading. In fact, I would caution any potential CFD traders from using the following information as a definitive guide. No two successful traders use exactly the same approach. Successful trading is a combination of basic trading techniques, a disciplined mental approach and an understanding of your own trading personality.

Your trading personality is a combination of your instinctive preferences and your conscious desires. Every trading personality is therefore unique. My intention is to provide a number of trading concepts and strategies, and for readers to make use of the ideas that resonate.

Choosing the Right CFD to Trade

Your CFD provider should offer the full range of top stocks on the underlying exchange. These stocks might not necessarily be the most volatile and they certainly won't be the cheapest, but they do provide a degree of liquidity. Liquidity is important because this directly affects the width of the spread. A stock with low liquidity can have a wide spread making it more expensive to trade, because each cent away from the last-traded price that is quoted adds a hidden cost to trade. CFD pricing is the same as the spread quoted on the underlying exchange, so the size of the spread quoted will directly affect the cost of trading the CFD.

Some stocks, despite their status as a top stock, may suffer from a wide spread. This is common with companies where employees are also shareholders. For example, Flight Centre (FLT) is a top 100 stock on the ASX, but because a large proportion of the outstanding shares are held by employees, a relatively small percentage of share capital is traded on a day-to-day basis. This can create a relatively wide spread. While most top Australian stocks will trade with a 1¢ or 2¢ spread, I have seen FLT with a spread of 10¢, 20¢, and even 50¢.

Spreads can also be affected by volatility. When rumours are circulating or unexpected news is released to the market, spreads can widen in the short term on stocks that normally trade with a 1¢ spread. Therefore, don't be surprised if you receive a wider spread in moments of high volatility. If you trade at market, you will find a similarly wide spread on the underlying product. I recommend you check the market depth information on the underlying market when you are trading CFDs. This shows how much volume is being demanded at the bid and being supplied at the offer. For instance, a large order to buy 100,000 share CFDs will not receive the bid and offer price quoted on the underlying exchange if the exchange only has an order of 10,000 shares at that offer price. The CFD provider will follow the exchange prices in respect to the orders on the underlying exchange.

Some of the most popular share CFDs on the ASX are News Corporation Limited (NCP), the big four banks, and the larger resource companies such as Rio Tinto Limited (RIO) and BHP Billiton Limited (BHP). However it is not just the larger stocks that present trading opportunities. Smaller top 200 stocks such as ERG Limited (ERG) and Croesus Mining NL (CRS) are also popular with CFD traders.

Before you choose which share CFD to trade, you should become very familiar with all the information available on the company and, in particular, the chart. If you are selling a CFD you should be aware of dividend dates because the cash equivalent will be deducted from your account (and added when buying a CFD). Reporting dates are also important because they can often be accompanied by extra volatility.

Market Analysis

Most people who trade CFDs are short-term traders looking to make profits in a matter of hours, days or weeks. For the short-term trader a low- or no-brokerage environment and the offer of online instant dealing are the essential tools to take advantage of fast market moves. Many experts in the past have declared it impossible to make money from day or short-term trading. Traditional share or futures dealing, where normal commission is charged, will make the broker a rich person, while leaving the trader poorer. Win, lose or breakeven, your account will be slowly eroded by paying transaction costs. Now that private investors have access to low-commission and commission-free trading, this is simply not true.

Stalking the Market

Because short-term trading takes advantage of day-to-day volatility, fundamentals can be of limited use. Successful short-term traders are masters of the 'tape', which means they understand the tick-by-tick price action of a stock or market. If you are preparing for a career as a short-term trader, then you must become a master of the price action. Studying historical data enables you to become familiar with the unique character of a stock or index. Detailed analysis of the chart will reveal important recurring features of the stock that are likely to appear again.

There is no substitute for watching live price action when you are getting to know your stock. Before you take your first trade, stalking the stock or market you are going to trade should be part of your preparation. The best approach is to select a limited number of stocks and get to know them intimately. Becoming familiar with price action allows you to comfortably wear loss-making price moves without exiting a trade that is eventually profitable. The day-to-day volatility is the double-edged sword of the short-term trader because it provides your money-making possibilities and at the same time serves as your biggest challenge to remain in a trade. Familiarity with price action will also help you understand and have the patience to enter a trade only when circumstances offer the best opportunity to make money, rather than chasing the market with the herd.

Stalking a stock involves more than just having a good knowledge of the recent price action. Good short-term trading analysis also includes a rock solid understanding of the long-term trends and medium-term outlook.

Analysis Checklist

Here is a checklist of questions that can help you gain more insight into the stock or market you are going to trade:

↳   What is the long-term, medium-term and short-term outlook for the stock or market and at what stage is it within this tend—beginning, middle or end?

↳   How have chart patterns formed?

↳   How has the stock reacted to general market-moving events?

↳   What is the trend for the sector in general and other key stocks in the sector?

↳ What is the trend for the general stock market and how is it performing in relation to that trend?

↳ What are the daily and weekly ranges?

↳ How does the stock react to previous support and resistance levels?

↳ Does the stock gravitate to particular retracements or numbers; for example, round numbers or Fibonacci levels?

IDENTIFYING THE TREND

The first challenge for the short-term trader is identifying the trend. Short-term trading can be undertaken at any stage in an uptrend. The popular approach is to buy low and sell high but, in reality, the middle stages of an uptrend can be easier to buy and often deliver faster profits than the early stages.

When zealous traders share their trading stories it is invariably about the stock that was purchased at historical lows for a mammoth profit rather than the sobering tale of a bottom-picking disaster. In reality, successful bottom-picking is so rare an occurrence you can expect to do it maybe once in a lifetime, if that. The biggest challenge for new traders is to re-program the buy low, sell high mentality.

One way to face reality is to review time and sales data. Time and sales data provided by the exchange gives tick-by-tick price action with times and volume executed. A significant reversal price usually trades on very small volume, sometimes only once, representing literally one buyer and one seller transacting at the price. Picking an exact turning point is more likely to be pure luck more than a special trading skill.

Not all stocks follow the format for an uptrend I have detailed below, but many do. Understanding this pattern makes your trading more predictable and, when the probability of an event occurring increases, your chance to make money also improves. Therefore, when you are looking for a stock to trade short term, save yourself the angst and stick to stocks that follow a common pathway. There are plenty of stocks that have historical price action that follows the norm and can be, therefore, highly tradeable using CFDs for short-term profits.

Early Stages of an Uptrend

The time between the end of a downtrend and the confirmation of a new uptrend is more often a matter of weeks, months or even years. The further a stock price has fallen from its highs, the longer it will generally take to reverse into a new uptrend. This is because buyers who have witnessed the process of losses grow increasingly more negative on a stock as it falls. As they exit the market and watch it fall further it reinforces their negative outlook on the stock. Buying activity slowly accumulates as new buyers see an opportunity and the cycle starts again.

New buying interest is usually cautious and reflected in a number of failed attempts to rally that result in more tests of the lows. This means the early stages of a sustainable uptrend usually follow a pattern of small ranges, with slow upside progress and a well-tested reversal point often represented by a double-, triple- or multiple-bottom pattern. An easy way to ascertain the sustainability of a potential reversal is to compare it to past rallies in the downtrend. If it looks similar, it will likely play out the same way and the downtrend will continue (see Chart 5.1, page 69).

Middle Stages of an Uptrend

The middle stages of an uptrend will show strong upside momentum as increasing numbers of buyers enter the market.

If the early stages of the uptrend represent uncertainty, the middle stages show steady resolve. Sideways trading at the beginning of the uptrend give way to the middle stages of an accelerating series of higher lows and higher highs.

The majority of the move involved in an uptrend usually occurs in the middle stages of the trend. It is also the time when you can expect the shortest corrections in terms of time and distance. For short-term traders this is the best time to go long. With minimal corrections and steady gains, the potential for stress-free and orderly profits is maximised. Looking at Chart 5.1 (opposite), after confirming the double-bottom pattern in May 2001, Metcash Trading Limited (MTT) set sail for higher ground, meeting limited resistance in the form of short-lived pullbacks.

Later Stages of an Uptrend

As buying reaches an exhaustion two things can happen in an uptrend. Firstly, the uptrend can make extremely sharp gains as an emotional element enters the market and Johnny-come-lately investors rush in as an effort not to miss out. Therefore, the later stages of an uptrend can be characterised by almost straight-line gains that, in hindsight, always look unsustainable.

Secondly, the end phase of an uptrend can also show the first signs of the downtrend that will follow. Wide swings following a good run higher can be the first sign of the end. This gives rise to double- or triple-top patterns where a multiple-tested reversal point represents profit-taking and evaporating buying interest. The chart for MTT demonstrates the late stages of the uptrend when it made straight-line gains in April and May 2002.

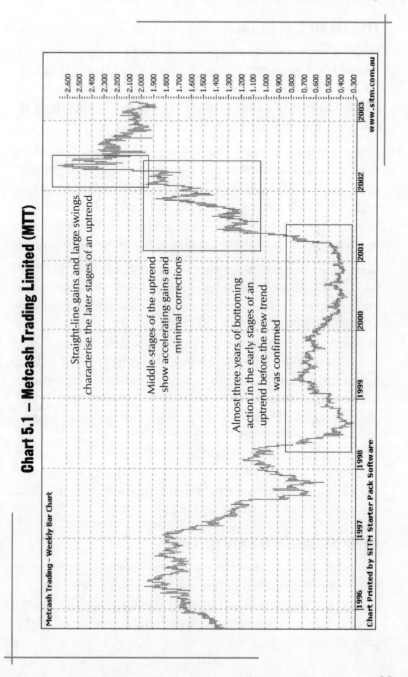

Chart 5.1 – Metcash Trading Limited (MTT)

Metcash Trading – Weekly Bar Chart

Straight-line gains and large swings characterise the later stages of an uptrend

Middle stages of the uptrend show accelerating gains and minimal corrections

Almost three years of bottoming action in the early stages of an uptrend before the new trend was confirmed

Chart Printed by SITM Starter Pack Software

www.sitm.com.au

The Dead Cat Bounce

When a market rallies sharply in the midst of a downtrend it is known as a 'dead cat bounce'. Beware of the dead cat bounce, for it is also known as a bear market trap. Investors thinking the downtrend has ended rush back into the market, only to find the rally ends abruptly.

Investors trying to trade the dead cat bounce are mauled by the ferocious downturn that occurs when the buying pressure dries up. A dead cat bounce at the beginning of a downtrend will look like a resumption of the uptrend and tempt many bargain-hunters to buy. As the downtrend progresses the incidence and size of the dead cat bounce generally recede.

What does this mean for short-term traders? The dead cat bounce is a powerful attraction for traders looking for quick profits. However, the problem with the dead cat bounce is its unpredictability. They can take hold in a day, last a few days or weeks and return to the lows and beyond in even less time. My rule with a dead cat bounce is don't buy it. They are indeed a trap for buyers and are, ironically, a much better tool for short-term selling since they signal more significant losses ahead. Since CFDs have made shorting the market so simple, a dead cat bounce can now be regarded as a signal of an upcoming opportunity to short the market, rather than go long and second-guess a rally. The chart for Lihir Gold Limited (LHG) shows the downtrend containing three dramatic dead cat bounces (see Chart 5.2, opposite).

Early Stages of a Downtrend

When an uptrend is over it can take many months or sometimes years of price action to confirm the fact. If that wasn't the case, then everybody would sell when a market tops. The key to identifying the early stages of a downtrend is to understand the price action that has preceded it.

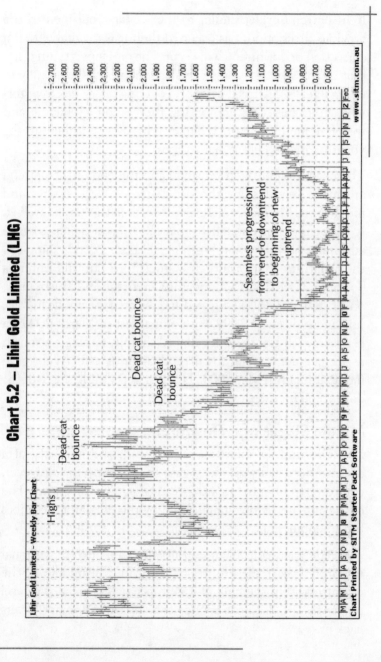

Chart 5.2 – Lihir Gold Limited (LHG)

Lihir Gold Limited – Weekly Bar Chart

Highs

Dead cat bounce

Dead cat bounce

Dead cat bounce

Seamless progression from end of downtrend to beginning of new uptrend

Chart Printed by SITM Starter Pack Software

www.sitm.com.au

If an uptrend cycle, similar to the scenario outlined in the previous description, has occurred then it is inevitable that a correction or downtrend will occur. The problem is timing, and that is why so many 'top pickers' lose money. When a rally in the market is described as 'short covering', it means investors with short positions are exiting the market by buying and therefore forcing the price higher. This can contribute to the volatility that occurs at market tops.

The beginning of the downtrend and the end of the uptrend are made seamless by the incidence of large swings and multi-tested highs. Not all reversals occur in this way. However, it happens often enough to make it a great signal to take advantage of with a short position. Telstra is a good example of the volatility that occurs as a stock tops out and enters a downtrend (see Chart 5.3, opposite). From the $9.20 highs made on 1 February 1999, TLS tested and rejected the upside in May, July and November 1999, with a final test in March 2000. In between each test the price dipped sharply, retracing as much as 22 per cent. The downtrend did not effectively gain momentum until May 2000. TLS was in the early stages of the downtrend for over a year.

Middle Stages of a Downtrend

Like the middle stages of an uptrend, the maturity of a downtrend usually shows a gain in momentum. However, compared to an uptrend, moves can be significantly faster. The old saying 'up by the stairs, down by the escalator' describes this phenomenon.

The early stages of a downtrend are when the smart professional investors take their profits. It is during the middle of the downtrend that the bulk of investors exit. As the downtrend progresses the dead cat bounce can appear and tempt buyers back in.

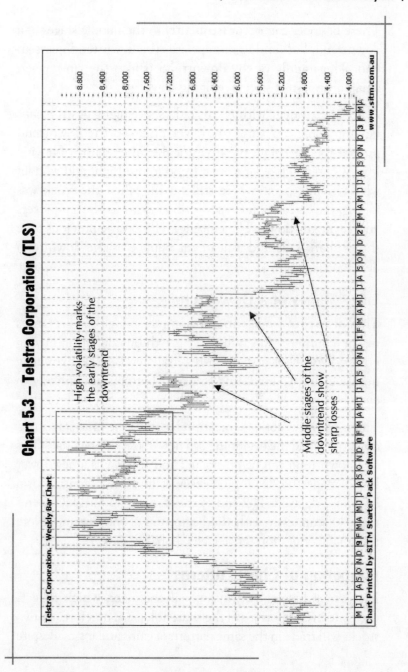

Chart 5.3 – Telstra Corporation (TLS)

Telstra Corporation. – Weekly Bar Chart

High volatility marks the early stages of the downtrend

Middle stages of the downtrend show sharp losses

Chart Printed by SITM Starter Pack Software

www.sitm.com.au

73

These bounces can occur frequently in the middle stages of a downtrend, but tend to disappear as the downtrend nears an end. The middle of the downtrend is also the time when amateur investors start 'averaging down'.

A popular strategy with retail traders, averaging down means buying a stock at variously lower prices as the downtrend progresses. This gives the investor the false feeling of buying low. When you look at a downtrend in hindsight and wonder why so many people were still buying when the stock was falling, you can attribute most of that buying to bottom-pickers and averaging down. The chart for TLS on the previous page shows sharp falls and a dead cat bounce as the downtrend developed.

Later Stages of a Downtrend

The last gasps of the downtrend show increasingly smaller ranges in the counter-trend rallies. This exhibits deflating buying power. Sentiment at bottom reversals tends to be extremely negative, and you will find stocks at bottoms are unlikely to even be covered by the research department of your broker.

There is a very subtle delineation between the final stages of a downtrend and the beginning of a new uptrend. The final stages of a downtrend can be protracted and as soon as a new lower low is made the downtrend resumes and the potential for a bottom is delayed. The end of the downtrend for LHG seems to meld seamlessly with the beginning of the uptrend. Note the small congestion range (see Chart 5.2, page 71).

Formation of Chart Patterns

Each stock has its own individual character, which reflects the collective emotions of the shareholders. Therefore, no two stocks will trade in the same pattern of gains and losses, despite being part of the same general movement in the stock market. While the generic patterns of uptrends and downtrends are the basis of your analysis, it is the specific way in which a stock manifests these patterns that is crucial to mastering the stocks you will short-term trade with CFDs. For instance, a gap on a chart generally implies a continuation of the trend, or when it appears towards the end of a trend may be an upcoming reversal. The chart for Rio Tinto Limited (RIO) is a good example of a chart that is littered with gaps (see Chart 5.4, overleaf). A gap on its own has little meaning on this RIO chart.

An important step towards determining the character of a stock is to review all the common chart patterns that have occurred in its past. This means asking questions such as:

↳ How did this stock start a new uptrend?

↳ How did it trade towards the end of the uptrend?

↳ Does it trade double-bottom patterns? And, if so;

↳ Do they generally reach their target or do they go well beyond?

Short-term trading means having a visual knowledge of the price action for a particular stock. It means understanding it like the proverbial 'back of your hand'.

Performance in Relation to External Situations and Events

How a stock reacts to market-moving events can indicate future price action. For instance, the September 11, 2001 World Trade Center disaster sent the Australian stock market into a severe dip, followed by an even stronger rally back to all-time highs. If a stock did not rally in accordance with the general market following the September event, then this was an early warning sign of weakness.

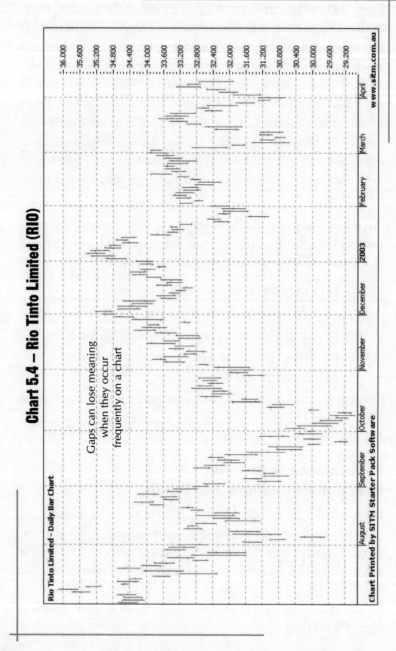

Chart 5.4 – Rio Tinto Limited (RIO)

Gaps can lose meaning when they occur frequently on a chart

AMP Limited (AMP) is a good example of a stock that demonstrated weakness following the event. As the general market rallied into new highs in early 2001, AMP made a high at $22. The September 11, 2001 event was especially detrimental to the insurance sector. AMP fell to a low of $16.35, and the post-September 11 rally took the price to $19.76. More significant was the price action following this high. Only three months later, in June 2002, AMP had closed below its September 2001 lows, which indicated the market was more negative about AMP than at the time of the September 11, 2001 event. At the same time, the S&P/ASX 200 Index was 11 per cent above its September lows and another key stock in the sector, QBE Insurance (QBE), was trading more than 100 per cent above its September 2001 lows. These comparisons can give you extra insight into the underlying sentiment for a stock (see Chart 5.5, overleaf).

Daily and Weekly Ranges

When you are a short-term trader using a leveraged product, the biggest challenge is staying in a trade when the position moves against you. Because returns are magnified, the move in the underlying will bring even greater impact to your account. It is important to review the daily and weekly ranges for a stock. This will allow you to gauge the volatility you can expect to encounter as you hold the CFD position and how quickly the trade will move to your target. A low volatility stock will probably give you minimal concern if the price moves against you, but will also take longer to reach your target. This can be advantageous if your trading strategy is to take large positions with small profit targets. The daily and weekly range for a stock can determine if a stock is suitable to trade in light of your trading personality. This information can also indicate how you would tailor your strategy based on these trading ranges.

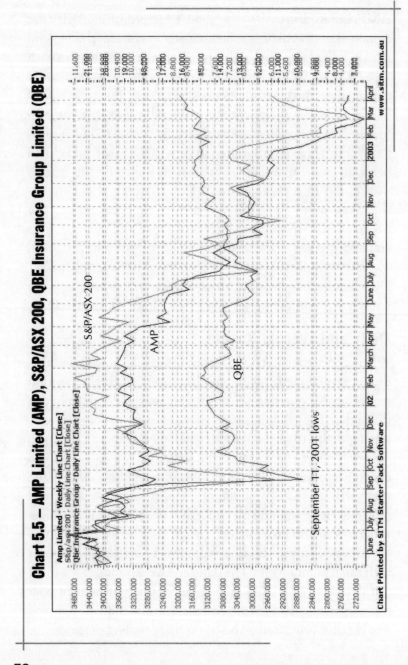

Chart 5.5 – AMP Limited (AMP), S&P/ASX 200, QBE Insurance Group Limited (QBE)

Amp Limited – Weekly Line Chart [Close]
S&p/asx 200 – Daily Line Chart [Close]
Qbe Insurance Group – Daily Line Chart [Close]

S&P/ASX 200

AMP

QBE

September 11, 2001 lows

Chart Printed by SITM Starter Pack Software

www.sitm.com.au

Retracement Levels

When trading with a short-term focus, every possible area of support and resistance of the chart becomes important. Old peaks and troughs on the chart are the most obvious points on the chart for further extensions of the trend to pause or reverse. However, another common tool for finding support and resistance is the calculation of Fibonacci levels.

The Fibonacci number sequence was discovered by the Italian mathematician Leonarda Pisana (known as Fibonacci), who was also credited with bringing the decimal number system to the Latin-speaking world.

In his book *Liber Abaci*, published in 1202, Fibonacci introduced the number sequence of integers expressed as:

1, 1, 2, 3, 5, 8, 13, 21, 34, 55, . . . (infinity)

The sum of any two adjacent numbers creates the next higher number sequence. For example:

$$1 + 1 = 2$$
$$1 + 2 = 3$$
$$2 + 3 = 5$$
$$3 + 5 = 8$$

The ratios of any two numbers in sequence (after the first four numbers) approaches 1.618, creating a logarithmic growth spiral. Accordingly, the reverse relationship creates the inverse— 0.618. These two ratios, 1.618 and 0.618, are known as the 'golden mean'.

The golden mean is more than just a mathematical quirk. The logarithmic spiral describes a growth pattern seen throughout the universe. For example the number of branches on a tree increases each year in the ratio of successive Fibonacci numbers. The human body is in Fibonacci proportion, and Fibonacci relationships are found in everything from shells and flowers to galaxies. The sequence was also known to the ancient Greeks and Egyptians, and used to construct the Parthenon and the Great Pyramid of Gizah. The numbers are now recognised as a natural harmony that manifests in all human creative achievement including art, architecture, and music. Therefore, it is not surprising that the golden mean should be applied to the sharemarket, since it represents one of the purest forms of mass human behaviour.

In trading terms, the most important quality of the sequence is the golden mean. However, there are other special qualities of the number sequence:

↳ The relationship between every second number in sequence is 2.618 or the inverse 0.382

↳ 0.618 squared equals 0.382

↳ 1 minus 0.618 equals 0.382

↳ 1.618 multiplied by 0.618 equals 1

↳ 0.382 multiplied by 0.618 equals 0.236.

These numbers are commonly quoted as two-digit percentages (62 per cent, 38 per cent, and so on). It is also possible to derive 50 per cent from the Fibonacci numbers since the first two numbers in sequence can be rationalised to produce 0.50. This is commonly used when calculating Fibonacci levels.

Some stocks will frequently gravitate to Fibonacci ratio retracements, while these levels might appear to have no significance on the charts of other stocks. How a stock will react to key Fibonacci levels can help you identify a reversal point or even gauge the strength of a trend. Part of your analysis should be the identification of past and potential Fibonacci retracement levels. This will alert you to possible upcoming turning points or pauses in the trend. Most charting packages will have a Fibonacci tool which means there are no calculations to make.

BHP Billiton Limited (BHP) has reversed on Fibonacci retracement levels on numerous occasions. One of those Fibonacci retracements was the major reversal low of late-1998. Based on the distance from the 1987 lows to the highs of 1997, BHP made a low at $4.84, just 4¢ away from the Fibonacci 62 per cent retracement level of $4.88 (see Chart 5.6, overleaf).

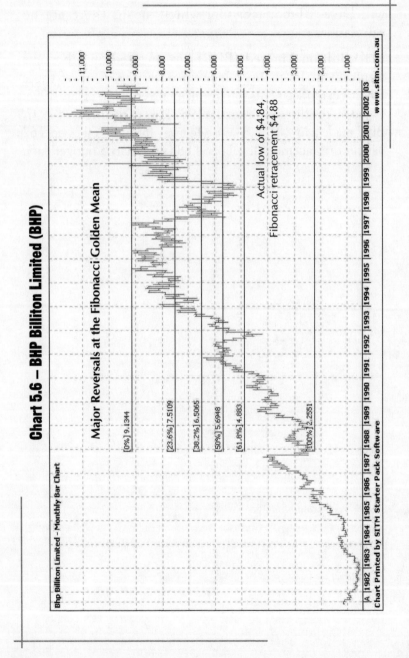

Chart 5.6 – BHP Billiton Limited (BHP)

Bhp Billiton Limited – Monthly Bar Chart

Major Reversals at the Fibonacci Golden Mean

[0%] 9.1344

[23.6%] 7.5109

[38.2%] 6.5065

[50%] 5.6948

[61.8%] 4.883

Actual low of $4.84,
Fibonacci retracement $4.88

[100%] 2.2551

Chart Printed by SITM Starter Pack Software

www.sitm.com.au

chapter 6

SHORT-TERM TRADING TECHNIQUES AND STRATEGIES

Reversal Days and Spikes

Reversal Day

A top reversal day occurs when the price trades higher than the previous session, but closes lower than the previous day's close. A bottom reversal is the opposite—a lower low than the previous day and a higher close. Figure 6.1 (overleaf) shows a top reversal day and a bottom reversal day.

A reversal day is more likely to herald a change of trend if the session range is wide and made on heavier volume. If the range exceeds the extremes of the previous day it is called an outside day. A reversal day may not spell the end of a trend, but it usually provides a good indication of a short- to medium-term reversal of trend.

Two-Day Reversal

The price action of a reversal day can be made over two days and is known as a two-day reversal. For a top reversal, day one shows a new high and a close at the highs. On day two, the price opens near the previous day's close but does not continue higher and instead closes at or below the previous low (see Figure 6.2, opposite). For a bottom reversal, the market makes a lower low but closes near the highs of the previous session highs. A reversal day is important only if it occurs after a developed trend has occurred. The steeper the trend, the more likely the reversal day will cause a pause or reversal in trend.

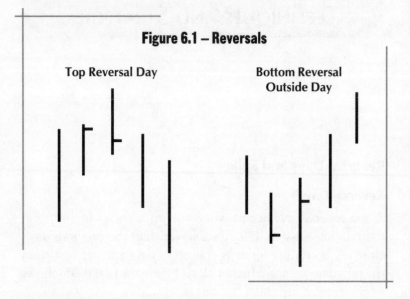

Figure 6.1 – Reversals

Top Reversal Day

Bottom Reversal Outside Day

The Spike

The spike is also known as a 'V' formation and is a very large range day that appears at either market bottoms or tops. A spike top shows a large range of price action above the previous day's trading range. A spike bottom is the opposite (see Figure 6.2, opposite). The spike top does not necessarily form on a higher open and a lower close and, similarly, a spike bottom does not have to finish on its highs. However, a spike made on a reversal day makes it more significant. Spike tops are more likely to produce a major reversal of trend than a spike bottom but there are exceptions to the rule.

Figure 6.2 – Reversals

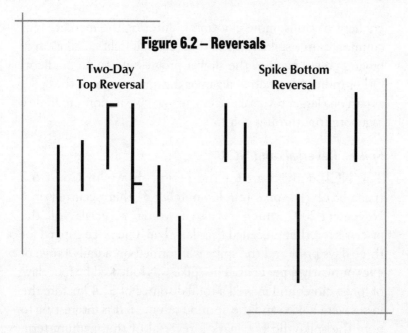

Two-Day
Top Reversal

Spike Bottom
Reversal

Chart 6.1 (on page 87) of Westpac Banking Corporation Limited (WBC) shows a number of spikes in the uptrend that did not eventuate in a long-term reversal. Spike reversals are sudden and can move dramatically into a new trend in a short period of time. This makes them difficult to trade since a slow-moving reversal is much easier to catch in the early stages.

A spike can occur on an island reversal—where the price gaps before and after the turning point—or on a key reversal. A reversal day occurs either in a single trading session or over a period of two sessions. In a single session bearish reversal the price trades higher than the previous session and then closes at a lower close than the previous session.

A spike on its own is not enough reason to take a short-term trade. Other conditions must exist to make the spike significant. An accelerating trend is a good precursor for a spike. As an uptrend develops and extends itself above the previous gradient of gains, more emotion is entering the market. This culminates in a spike reversal that sees a dramatic deflation of buying power back to the slower progressing trend gradient. Other indicators, such as a gap or the appearance of the spike as part of a larger reversal pattern, would give it more credibility as a potential turning point.

Spikes, Reversals and NCP

The NCP daily chart for the period shown in Chart 6.2 (page 88) has a spike (circled number 3) that occurred on 6 November 2002, which was also a two-day reversal. Note the price action that preceded this daily bar. The price gapped for three days prior and the spike was formed on a daily range of 49¢, or nearly 4 per cent. The spike was followed by four days of lower closes and moved a total distance of $1.49 before the losses were halted and the uptrend resumed. It is interesting to note the spike did not mark a reversal of the medium-term trend.

If a spike bottom were to form on a low in the recent range it would give more weight to a buy signal. The spike bottom that occurred on 11 March was preceded by a series of gap down-days, culminating in a low of $9.19 and a high, open and close at $9.49. The following day's price action gapped open, filled the gap and closed higher, giving further credence that this was an important reversal day.

From the sample of price history under study, the NCP chart shows spike reversals at bottoms are more common than at tops. I have also noted that of the six short- and medium-term tops on the NCP chart, including the highs of August (1), September (2), November (3), December (4), January (5) and February (6), the reversal bar included a relatively large range, making new highs or at least new closing highs, with a close high in the range on all occasions.

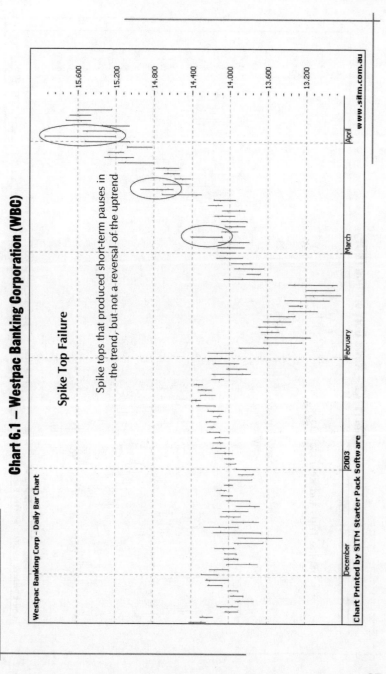

Chart 6.1 – Westpac Banking Corporation (WBC)

Westpac Banking Corp – Daily Bar Chart

Spike Top Failure

Spike tops that produced short-term pauses in the trend, but not a reversal of the uptrend

Chart Printed by SITM Starter Pack Software

www.sitm.com.au

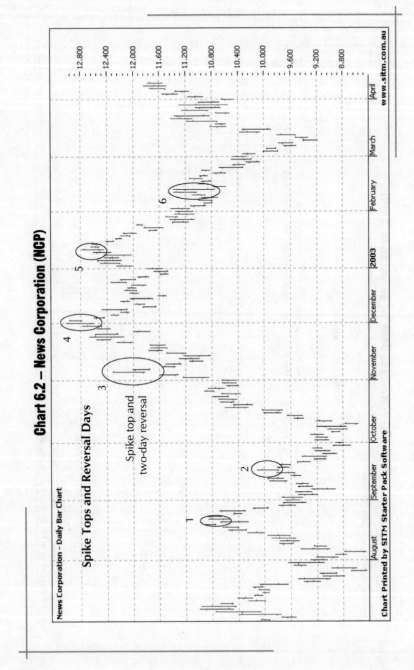

Chart 6.2 – News Corporation (NGP)

News Corporation – Daily Bar Chart

Spike Tops and Reversal Days

Spike top and
two-day reversal

www.sitm.com.au

Chart Printed by SITM Starter Pack Software

Trading NCP with Spikes and Reversals

From the study of reversals and spikes on the NCP chart it is possible to discern two potential trading strategies (buy NCP and sell NCP), both of which will be outlined over the next two pages.

Buy NCP

The suggested entry rules outlined below mean the three medium-term bottom reversals on the NCP chart were buy signals. The rules for an NCP bottom, based on a spike/reversal, are:

↳ Formation of a spike bottom that is also a reversal day (close must be at top of day's trading range).

↳ A gap open before the spike bottom (but can be filled) and a gap open on the day following the spike (which can also be filled).

Profit Target

The spike and reversal day does not pin-point a profit target for the trend, but it does hint that the wider these phenomena, the further the trend should travel. The best profit target to use in these situations is to employ one of the methods of the trailing stop (this will be explained later in the chapter).

Stop-loss

The beauty of this approach is the ability to identify an exact stop-loss level. You could exit this trade if the low of the spike was breached on a closing basis. However, the chart suggests the trade will fail and should be exited if it is not showing a profit by the end of day one.

Sell NCP

The reversal day pattern is not a common feature of the NCP chart for the period shown. However, there were only two spike tops on the NCP chart and both of those resulted in a change of trend and good profit potential from the move that followed over the next few days.

The first, the high of 17 September (2), was a higher spike formed in a downtrend, which already makes it a safer opportunity to sell. On the day after the spike, the price opened on a gap down, rallied to a high of 2¢ into the range of the previous day, but finished lower. It then continued lower until it made major lows on 10 October.

With the high of 6 November (3), note the large range rising bars of the two days prior to this top. Either of these bars could potentially be the turnaround for NCP. However, the open of the day following 6 November was the key—it was significantly lower in the range of the previous day. The other two potential spikes were followed by higher gap opens.

Profit Target

Take profit on a trailing stop (explained later in this chapter) or wait for a bottom reversal pattern.

Stop-loss

Use the top of the spike high as the initial stop-loss, but as for the buy signal, exit if the position is not in profit at end of day one.

TRADING SUPPORT AND RESISTANCE

The idea of support and resistance is one of the foundation concepts of technical analysis. Therefore, a powerful trading approach can be based on this crucial concept, by going long at a close above resistance and going short at a close below support. When you fully grasp the idea of support and resistance, then the strategy of selling at a low and buying at a high seems not only obvious, but prudent. The theory of buy high and sell low is part of the old rule 'the trend is your friend'. On a short-term basis with the ability to go long or short, buying high and selling low can deliver very fast profits and provide some good mechanical signals for entry, exit and stop-loss. Trading support and resistance is also one of simplest technical trading approaches.

What is Support and Resistance?

On the charts the troughs are called support, and represent levels under the market where buying interest is stronger than selling pressure and a decline in prices is halted. The peaks are called resistance, and represent the reverse or levels above the market where selling pressure is stronger than buying interest and a price rise is halted. The significance of a support or resistance level increases with the amount of time and the number of incidents the price tests and rejects the level. The weekly chart of NCP shows all highs and lows marked with 'R' for resistance and 'S' showing support (see Chart 6.3, overleaf). Multiple-tested levels are represented with a line drawn under the price action for a support level or above for a resistance level.

Old Highs and Lows

The most obvious support or resistance level on a chart is a previous high or low. The failure to violate a previous peak in an uptrend, or the inability of prices to go below the previous support in a downtrend, can be the first warning sign that the existing trend is changing.

Round Numbers

Round numbers tend to act as natural support and resistance levels. A good example of round number resistance is the all-time high of NCP at exactly $28, highlighted on Chart 6.3. It is human nature for investors to target these numbers and for them to become turning points. These points on the chart are psychological levels, and knowing their significance can give an investor an important advantage.

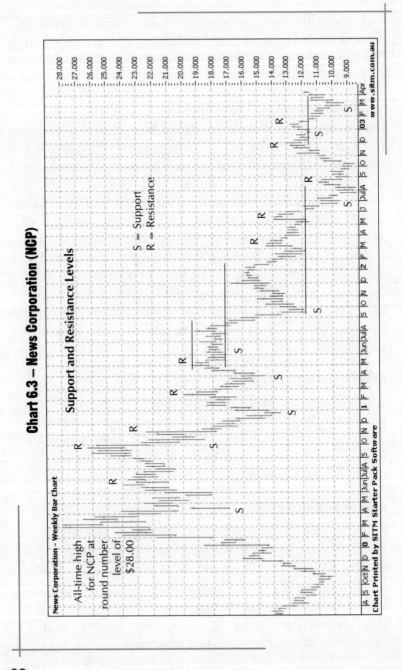

News Corporation - Weekly Bar Chart

Chart 6.3 – News Corporation (NCP)

Support and Resistance Levels

All-time high for NCP at round number level of $28.00

S = Support
R = Resistance

Chart Printed by SITM Starter Pack Software

www.sitm.com.au

When planning to enter or exit the trade, orders can be placed as the round number is approached, rather than directly at the number. It is a good policy to avoid round numbers since their popularity as trading targets means prices get near them but may never actually trade there, or do so on small volume.

Support and Resistance Reverse Roles

Support and resistance become interchangeable. This means that a resistance level, once breached, has the potential to act as support. This is also true for resistance. The multi-tested support level on Chart 6.4 (page 95) shows how these levels can reverse roles.

Buy Above Resistance

If resistance represents the price at which buyers are unwilling to pay for a stock and sellers see the means to make profits, then a close above a resistance level says there has been a change in that sentiment. Buyers now see value, and potential sellers are happy to maintain their long positions. The more times a resistance level is tested and rejected before finally being breached, the larger the move that is likely to follow. This is because as a level is tested, buying and selling power rises to meet each other and become equal—hence the price does not progress higher. Each time a resistance level is tested the battle between buyers and sellers starts again. The net effect is an accumulation of tension around these levels. When the price finally breaks above a resistance level it represents a release of pressure. Like a balloon that has burst, the more air it contains the further it will travel before all the air is gone and it stops moving.

Entry Points

Closing levels are the key for buying above resistance. However, the closing level will differ, depending on your timeframe.

If you are a short-term trader using daily charts, then the daily close price is your trigger to enter a trade. For an intraday or very short-term trader you will be using charts with much shorter price bars; for example, 15 or 30 minutes. As per the section above that describes the identification process of a trend, mid-trend price moves tend to provide the largest and fastest moves. Hence, the foundation for your support and resistance trading approach is a good understanding of the stage of the trend. A clear short position, based on a break of multi-tested support, occurred on the NCP chart on 28 January. The price closed below the $11.47 lows. Selling on the open of the following day would have given an entry at $11.37.

Profit Target

The idea of trading with the trend on a break-out of support or resistance is to ride that trend until the next level of support or resistance is reached. A popular charting technique to project the destination, following a break of support or resistance, is to take the vertical distance of the previous correction and add this measure to the break-out point for an uptrend and deduct for a downtrend.

For instance, on the NCP daily chart (Chart 6.4, opposite) if a short position were initiated on a close below the $11.47 support level, first take the distance of the rebound prior to the breakdown. This was $1.31 based on the move from $11.47 to $12.78. Then deduct $1.31 from $11.47 to get the first downside target at $10.15. In reality, the price moved much lower, but having a minimum target helps you to gauge the feasibility of a trade before it is entered into. This exercise also supplies a point from which you can narrow your stop-loss levels and protect your profits.

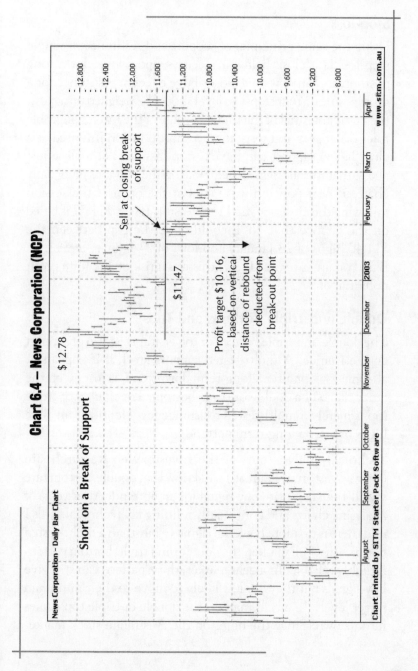

Chart 6.4 – News Corporation (NCP)

News Corporation - Daily Bar Chart

Short on a Break of Support

$12.78

Sell at closing break of support

$11.47

Profit target $10.16, based on vertical distance of rebound deducted from break-out point

www.sitm.com.au

Chart Printed by SITM Starter Pack Software

Stop-loss

Using the same principles of support and resistance, a simple stop-loss is a close below a recent support level for a long position and an exit on a close above a recent resistance for a short position. Your stop-loss level should be weighed up against the profit potential of the trade. Because of the interchangeable roles of support and resistance, a short position initiated at a close below support can have a stop-loss level at a close just above that initial trigger level. Note on the previous NCP daily chart, a short position was taken at the open of the session following the close above $11.47. A stop-loss at $11.57 is based on the chance that NCP could close the gap between the $11.40 highs of 28 January and lows of 23 January at $11.55. Based on an entry at $11.37, this was a risk of 20¢ for a profit potential of $1.21.

Double and Triple Bottoms and Tops

The double and triple bottom or top is simply a form of support and resistance. A multi-tested support level, if it appears at all-time lows or after a long-term downtrend, is just given the fancy name of a double or triple bottom. The double or triple top is merely a multi-tested resistance level found at all-time highs or after a long-term uptrend.

Technical analysis fans of the InvestorWeb Research site (www.investorweb.com.au) will know that double bottoms are my all-time favourite buy signal for an uptrend. After years of analysing charts and continually refining my technical skills I find there is no more powerful signal to buy than a multi-tested bottom. In a bull market, the double- and triple-bottom pattern is highly reliable. In a bear market, these pattern can still give buy signals but they are less likely to move to their minimum target levels. In a bear market, the double or triple top comes into its own. Since the highs on the Australian stock market of February 2002 double-top patterns have become a common and highly reliable event.

Pattern Confirmation is Crucial

Just because a bottom support level is hit twice does not make it a double-bottom pattern. The pattern is not confirmed until the price closes above the intervening high of the two lows. Figure 6.3 (below) illustrates the buy signal for a double bottom and the confirmation of the double-top pattern. A triple bottom or top merely implies another test of the extreme before the intervening level is breached. The breach must occur on a closing basis to confirm the pattern.

The short trade for NCP outlined previously was a sell on a break of support. This was, in effect, the confirmation of a double-top pattern, based on the highs of $13.02 and $12.78.

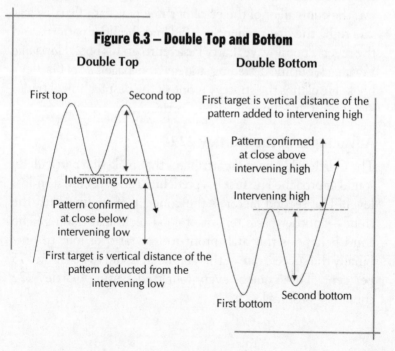

Figure 6.3 – Double Top and Bottom

Double Top

Double Bottom

First top

Second top

First target is vertical distance of the pattern added to intervening high

Intervening low

Pattern confirmed at close above intervening high

Pattern confirmed at close below intervening low

Intervening high

First target is vertical distance of the pattern deducted from the intervening low

Second bottom

First bottom

Double Top and Bottom Target

An upside target for a double-bottom pattern is based on the vertical distance of the pattern. Take this distance and add to the high of the pattern to get the first target. Take the distance of the double-top pattern and deduct from the low of the pattern for a downside target.

The longer it takes for a double-bottom pattern to form, the further it is likely to travel when it breaks. A new uptrend may take years to confirm a double-bottom pattern and the resultant uptrend can last even longer.

THE GARTLEY 222

Well before Gann or Elliott came to fame, M. Gartley wrote a book called *Profits in the Stock Market*. According to legend, Gartley's book was sold in the 1930s for US$1,500 a copy, which was the equivalent of the price of three new cars. Gartley was said to be the first to identify head and shoulder patterns and the reverse point wave. Larry Pesavento, in his book *Harmonic Vibrations*, outlines a trading strategy from page 222 of Gartley's book. He claims the strategy is one of the best technical trades ever found. It is known as the Gartley 222.

Advantages of the Gartley 222

The Gartley 222 has four attributes that make it a particularly sound approach. The first is a predefined and specific stop-loss level. The second factor is the concept of trading with the trend—another basic tenant of good technical trading. The third benefit is the high profit-to-loss ratio of four to one. Finally the success rate of this approach is said to be around 75 per cent. Three out of every four trades using Gartley 222 should be profitable.

How the Gartley 222 Pattern Works

The Gartley 222 pattern can be used in either bull or bear markets on intraday, daily, weekly or monthly charts, signalling both buy and sell orders. Figure 6.4 (below) shows the outline of a Gartley 222 buy and sell. A buy signal is given when an upward-trending market completes a correction back to point 'D'. A sell signal is produced when a downward-trending market completes a correction back to point 'D'. The trend reverses at 'A' and then corrects in three waves labelled 'B', 'C' and 'D'. You place an order to buy at point 'D', with a stop-loss under point 'X'. The opposite orders are placed for a falling market.

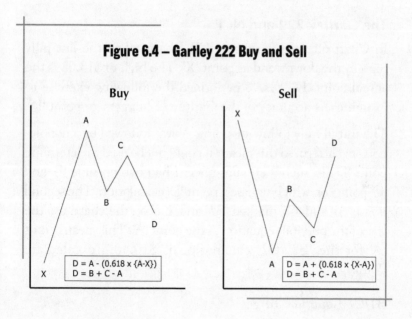

Figure 6.4 – Gartley 222 Buy and Sell

Buy

D = A - (0.618 x {A-X})
D = B + C - A

Sell

D = A + (0.618 x {X-A})
D = B + C - A

Determining Point 'D'

Point 'D' is calculated to find two possible turning points—a Fibonacci calculation of the distance of 'X' to 'A', and a level based on points 'A', 'B' and 'C'.

'D' as a Fibonacci level

Using the distance from 'X' to 'A', multiply by the Fibonacci golden mean—0.618. Deduct this amount from point 'A' for an uptrend and add it to point 'A' for a downtrend.

'D' as an ABC Equation

This is as straightforward as it appears. After the turning point 'A' is identified, wait for the development of a wave lower to 'B' and then another wave higher that stops short of point 'A', (i.e. point 'C'). Add the price of point 'B' to 'C' and then minus the price of point 'A'. This will give you point 'D'.

The Gartley 222 and NCP

In Chart 6.5 (opposite) of NCP, I have taken the last rally high in the downtrend as point 'X'. The high of $13.02 is the actual point 'D'. I have performed the following exercise to examine the accuracy of the Garltey 222 targets for point 'D'.

The initial rally following point 'A' was followed by a double-bottom pattern, so this meant it could not be used to determine point 'D'. In such a circumstance, I had two possible 'B' and 'C' points on which to base a point 'D' calculation. The second points 'B' and 'C', marked 'B2' and 'C2' on the chart, use the low of the previous equation as the point 'A'. This means point 'A' for the 'B2'/'C2' calculation is $10.40. To calculate Point D:

B1/C1 Equation Target

A = 8.44   B1 = 10.92   C1 = 10.40

D = B + C – A

D = 10.92 + 10.40 – 8.44 = 12.88

Chart 6.5 – News Corporation (NCP)

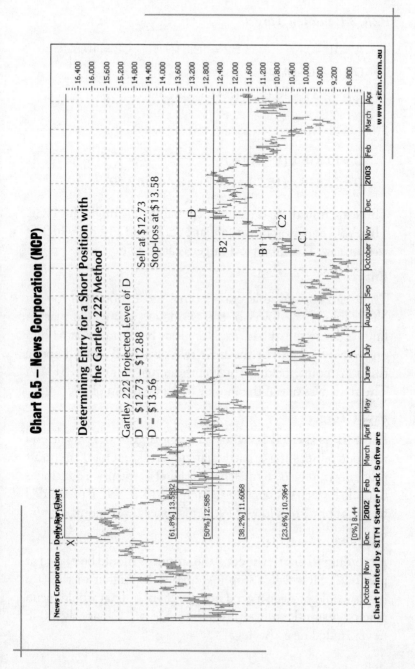

News Corporation - Daily Bar Chart

Determining Entry for a Short Position with
the Gartley 222 Method

Gartley 222 Projected Level of D

D = $12.73 – $12.88   Sell at $12.73
D = $13.56   Stop-loss at $13.58

[61.8%]13.3832
[50%]12.585
[38.2%]11.6068
[23.6%]10.3964
[0%]8.44

X

A

B1
B2
C1
C2
D

October Nov | Dec | 2002 | Feb | March | April | May | June | July | August | Sep | October | Nov | Dec | 2003 | Feb | March | Apr

Chart Printed by SITM Starter Pack Software

www.sitm.com.au

B2/C2 Equation Target

$A = 10.40$ $B2 = 12.31$ $C2 = 10.82$

$D = B + C - A$

$D = 12.31 + 10.82 - 10.40 = 12.73$

Fibonacci Target

$D = [0.618 \times (X - A)] + A$

$D = [0.618 \times (16.73 - 8.44)] + 8.44 = 13.56$

There are now three targets for a possible rally higher for NCP. The ABC equation targets are at $12.73 and $12.88, which is within 15¢. The Fibonacci target is at $13.56.

Entry

There are two possible entry points for a short position on NCP. Taking the lower of the two levels you would place a limit order to sell at $12.73. Note that NCP traded at $12.73 on 29 November. For the next two days NCP traded above this entry point, making a high at the actual point 'D' of $13.02. The trade was out of the money by a maximum of 29¢.

Profit Target

Point 'D' is the sell level for a resumption of the downtrend without prescribing a particular target. Therefore, the most prudent strategy is to trail the exit level as the price continues to trade lower. After making a high at $13.02, NCP proceeded to fall in price to a low of $9.19 just over three months later.

Stop-loss

According to Gartley theory, the stop-loss should be placed at point 'X'. However a stop-loss above the higher of the two levels would provide a good margin of error. That would mean placing a stop-loss level just above $13.56. Obviously, NCP never traded near this level.

Trading the Gap

When News Corporation opens 20¢, 50¢ or even $2.00 higher than the previous day, it has the capability of falling back just as fast and far. Gaps reflect volatility, and volatility is the essential ingredient for profitable short-term trading. Gap trading can give great mechanical trading signals.

How Does a Gap Form?

Gaps are places on the chart where no trading takes place. A gap occurs in an uptrend when the high of the preceding day is lower than the low of the following day—the opposite is true for a downtrend. For a gap to occur, investors have perceived an inaccurate estimation of value. Moreover, a gap is the equivalent to a time period of growing sentiment that does not manifest in price action.

Gaps of Importance

Not all gaps are important. Gaps that occur in thinly traded stocks are not significant. Gapping action is relative. A gap in a regularly gapping share price will not be worth scrutinising unless it is larger than the usual gap. Despite there being many gaps on the daily chart for NCP (on page 105), some of these provide important information on the state of the trend. There are four kinds of gaps: area, breakaway, runaway and exhaustion gaps.

Area Gap

Also known as a common gap, these gaps occur within a horizontal price congestion pattern on low volume. This kind of gapping action suggests that the market has little interest in the area between the extremes and therefore gives more significance to the extremes. Knowing this can help the investor identify a congestion or consolidation pattern, but it generally does not forecast the subsequent move.

Breakaway Gap

The breakaway gap generally forms at the completion of a period of accumulation in the form of a congestion pattern (often on an intraday basis) and signals the beginning of a significant price move. The occurrence of a conspicuous gap on the break-out of a price pattern implies the subsequent move would have more strength than a non-gapping break-out. The daily chart (opposite) for NCP has a number of breakaway gaps. This offers a very reliable opportunity to catch the early stages of a short-term trend in NCP.

Runaway Gap

The runaway gap initiates a second wave of trending action and generally follows a seemingly effortless and/or rapid advance or decline move. It is also known as a measuring gap because it heralds the halfway mark from the initial break-out to the next pause or ultimate reversal. Runaway gaps are not retraced until the market stages a significant reversal. This means runaway gaps offer good trading opportunities to trade with the trend. 'Go with the gap' should be your rule of thumb when trading a runaway gap.

On Chart 6.6, a good runaway gap trade was established when the price opened down 19¢ on 25 February. The trend was already conclusively downwards and the gap occurred around 80¢ from the breakaway gap that triggered the falls. Using the halfway-mark theory, the move from the open of $10.63 to the end of trend forecast a move of another 80¢. This gave a downside target at the high $9 mark. The falls that followed this move eventually rested at $9.19. Note that this gap was not filled for the remainder of the move lower.

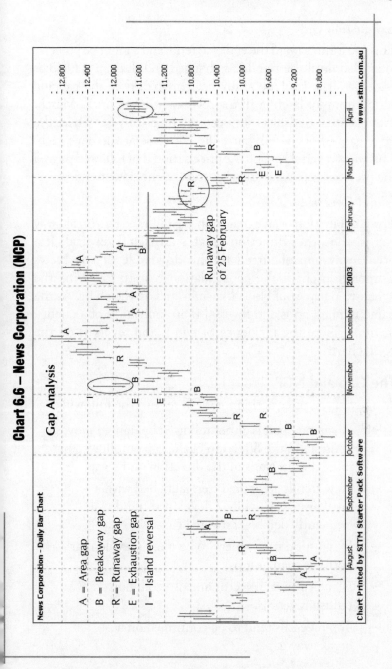

Chart 6.6 – News Corporation (NCP)

News Corporation - Daily Bar Chart

Gap Analysis

A = Area gap

B = Breakaway gap

R = Runaway gap

E = Exhaustion gap

I = Island reversal

Runaway gap
of 25 February

www.sitm.com.au

Chart Printed by SITM Starter Pack Software

Exhaustion Gap

This gap forms toward the end of a trend, and cannot be properly identified until the trend has changed and the gap is filled as prices reverse. Looking again at Chart 6.6, note the gapping action from 5 March until the reversal at $9.19 on 11 March. The eventual turning point occurred on a daily bar where the price gapped open, fell, but rallied to close at the day's high. This was a reversal bar and the price action that followed proved the previous gaps were an exhaustion of the downtrend.

Island Reversal

The combination of an exhaustion gap followed by a breakaway gap in the other direction creates an island reversal. If a breakaway gap occurred to the downside of the News Corporation chart, the consolidation pattern following the exhaustion gap would look like an island on the chart. As the name implies, an island reversal is an indication of a change in trend. Note the incidence of two island reversals on the NCP chart.

The Gap and NCP

A study of the price action for NCP reveals the following:

↳ A gap on open is either followed by limited moves contrary to the direction of the gap or followed by more serious gains in the direction of the gap.

↳ New trends are more often launched with a breakaway gap, while a developed trend will frequently demonstrate area gaps.

↳ Exhaustion gaps appear to be more prevalent at bottoms than at tops.

↳ Island reversal patterns are also common at bullish reversals.

↳ Top reversals tend to be confirmed on a breakaway gap.

Entry

Chart 6.7 (overleaf) suggests a breakaway gap on the downside would provide a good selling opportunity. However, not every downside breakaway gap resulted in a significant run lower. The ones that did result in a serious new downtrend were gap days that closed on their lows. Check the chart for the highlighted gap down bars. All were followed by a significant move lower. Therefore, your entry point for NCP is on the open of the following day after the gap day. A breakaway gap down occurred on 16 January. This is the most recent downside breakaway gap highlighted on the chart. The price opened at $12.39, following a low of the previous session at $12.50. A high at $12.42 failed to close the gap and the day's low and close were at $12.30. This gave a sell signal and, based on the next day's open, would have you take a short at $12.25. Another gap lower on the open of that day gave more confirmation for the short signal.

Profit Target

Minimum target for this move is the distance of the price action from the reversal highs to the low of the gap day, deducted from the low of the gap day. The high of 13 January was at $12.78. Deduct the difference between this level and the gap low of $12.30 to get a distance of 48¢. Now deduct this from $12.30 to get a first target at $11.82. NCP reached the minimum target just three days later when the price gapped at a price of $11.75.

Stop-loss

A stop-loss placed a few cents above the breakaway gap high covers a rebound in the new downtrend. The strongest rebound of the downtrend that was initiated with the breakaway gap of January 2003 was a high of $11.95. The stop-loss was a few cents above the breakaway gap day high of $12.42, reached on 24 January.

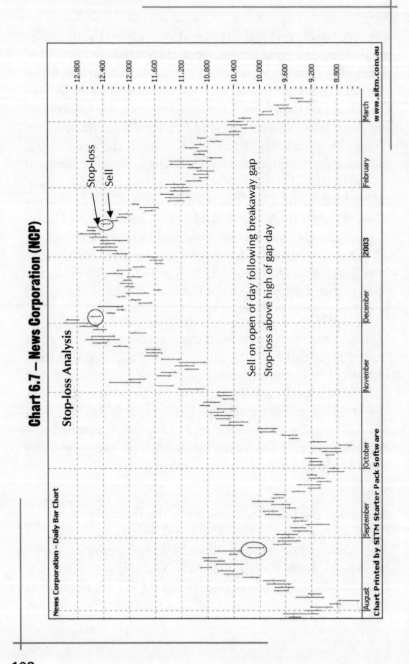

Chart 6.7 – News Corporation (NCP)

News Corporation – Daily Bar Chart

Stop-loss Analysis

Stop-loss

Sell

Sell on open of day following breakaway gap

Stop-loss above high of gap day

Chart Printed by SITM Starter Pack Software

www.sitm.com.au

BOLLINGER BANDS

In general, I am not a big fan of technical indicators. By indicators I mean the kinds of derivative calculations that give rise to measurements such as relative strength index, rate of change and stochastic. As the well-known Gann trader Bill McLaren once told me, they are like 'trying to trade shadows on a wall'. There are many experienced and successful traders who use indicators. However, for new zealous traders, indicators can create a kind of false confidence. They might provide nice buy and sell signals when overlaid on your historical data but in real time they are much more difficult to trade. For this reason I recommend you do not use them as your primary trading tool, but employ them in conjunction with the basics of trend, support and resistance and chart patterns.

What are Bollinger Bands?

Bollinger bands are represented as three lines overlayed on a daily bar chart. The centre line is a simple moving average, usually a 20-period. Two other lines run parallel to the centre line and will narrow and widen, depending on the trading activity. These two outer bands are two standard deviations of the moving average plotted above and below the central moving average line. Thus, Bollinger bands form an envelope around the price action. Bollinger bands are best used on an intermediate trend, hence 20 days, representing one month of trading days. However, this is not fixed, and some stocks will work better with another timeframe. Bollinger bands are meant to contain 95 per cent of the price action and for this reason alert the trader to any extremes in trading activity.

What is a Moving Average?

A moving average (MA) is calculated by taking a specified number of sequential closing prices of a stock or market, for example the last 20 days, adding them together and dividing by the number of periods. This single number is a trend-following device and, in its crudest form, is used as a buy signal when the price trades above its MA and a sell signal when the price trades below it.

Applying Bollinger Bands

Because of the mathematical calculation involved, Bollingers are not easy to draw by hand. Most good charting packages will have a Bollinger band tool (refer to Chart 6.8, opposite). The important features of Bollinger bands are:

↳ **Band width:** The distance between the upper and lower Bollinger band is important. Narrow band width implies low volatility and is usually followed by rapid and substantial price movement. Moreover the bands expand as the stock price becomes more volatile and contract as volatility falls.

↳ **Band extremes:** When the price moves to the upper band it is a sign of strength, while a move to the lower band represents a weakness in price.

↳ **Breaching the band:** When prices move outside the band you would, at first, expect the trend to continue. However, with each successive move outside the band, the greater the chance the price will reverse.

↳ **Price targets:** It is generally believed when a price move originates at one band, it will continue in that trend until it reaches the opposite band. Price reversals often occur at band extremes. This is based on the 95 per cent theory.

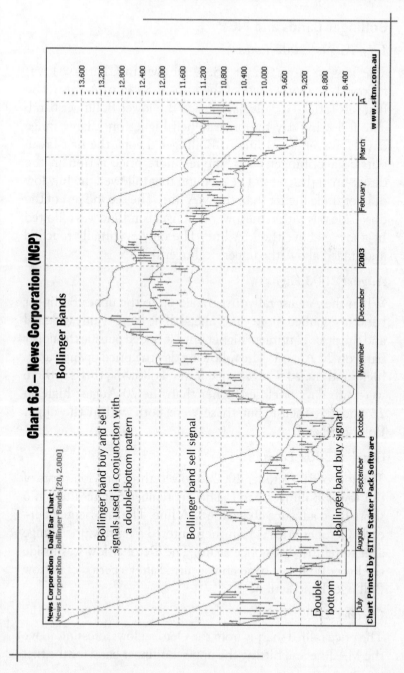

Chart 6.8 – News Corporation (NCP)

News Corporation - Daily Bar Chart
News Corporation - Bollinger Bands [20, 2.000]

Bollinger Bands

Bollinger band buy and sell
signals used in conjunction with
a double-bottom pattern

Bollinger band sell signal

Bollinger band buy signal

Double
bottom

Chart Printed by SITM Starter Pack Software

www.sitm.com.au

Bollinger Bands and NCP

July–August 2002 Lows

The low of July 2002 at $8.44 (shown in Chart 6.8) was followed by another test of the lows at $8.46 in August. The first test formed a daily bar outside the lower Bollinger band. The following day the price rallied higher on a large range day. However, according to Bollinger theory, the first break outside a Bollinger band implies more price action in the direction of the trend. The rebound that followed the July low did not trade higher than the MA line. The second test of the downside was within the lower Bollinger band and was followed by a move above the MA line. The rally eventually touched and traded above the upper Bollinger line.

August 2002 Highs

When the August rally first traded up to the upper Bollinger band it signalled more gains ahead. The band width widened and the price continued higher until it traded outside the upper band on 20 August. The following day the price opened at its highs and traded a large range lower. Following this day there were two days of closes higher than the 20 August high on 22 and 23 August, but these were both within the upper Bollinger band.

October 2002 Lows

The low of 10 October 2002 followed three previous tests of the lower Bollinger band. The September test resulted in a short-lived advance above the MA line. The late September–early October price action then entered a narrow price range as it tested the lows once again. The October low was inside the lower Bollinger band and occurred after a period of narrow Bollinger band action.

October 2002 Highs

The price rallied sharply from the October lows, crossing above the MA line and hitting the upper Bollinger band for the first time in mid-October. This implied a continuation of the rally. The high of 18 October was made on a bar outside the upper Bollinger band. On the day following, the price opened near its highs and traded lower, making a 22¢ range.

November 2002 Highs

After a short pause in the rally following the October highs, NCP made a spike top on 6 November. On the day following the highs, the price opened near its highs and closed at its lows trading a 26¢ daily range. The trade outside the upper Bollinger range implied more gains in the uptrend. A short-lived but steep decline continued to a low of $10.82 on 14 November. This traded briefly below the MA line, but by the following day the uptrend was back on track.

December 2002 Highs

As predicted by Bollinger theory, the price continued higher. The uptrend that started in August 2002 topped at a price of $13.02 on 2 December. From these highs the price fell, trading below the MA line but not touching the lower band of the Bollinger. This implied the correction that started at the $13.02 highs still had more downside.

January 2003 Highs

The second test of the $13.02 highs hugged the Bollinger band but failed to follow through to the upside, reaching a high of $12.78. The test of the upside also coincided with a narrowing of the bands, which according to Bollinger theory implied a break-out in price. The price once again closed below the MA line and a new downtrend started in earnest.

March 2003 Lows

The price stayed under the MA line until 14 March. The lows of 11 March occurred after a narrowing of the bands in late-February. From late-February, when the bands started to expand, there were 11 trading days before the trend reversed.

During that time, six of those days registered price action outside the lower Bollinger band.

Entry Point

Used as a confirming signal for a trade, the best Bollinger band signals occur on a breach of the MA line from a reversal on a Bollinger band extreme. Taking the July–August 2002 lows as a potential reversal; the price made a double-bottom pattern between $8.44 to an intervening high of $9.64 and back to a low of $8.46. Normally a double-bottom pattern on its own gives a buy signal when the price closes above the intervening high. However, the Bollinger bands gave an early warning sign that the short-term trend was to reverse.

The first test at $8.44 caused a breach of the lower Bolligner band, while the second test at $8.46 did not trade at or below the lower Bollinger—this was a non-confirmation of the downtrend. The same day the price closed above the intervening high of the double-bottom pattern. The price also traded above the MA. This gave a further confirmation of a new short-term uptrend.

Profit Target

The double-bottom target for the July–August lows was the distance of the pattern added to the high of the pattern. This gave a first upside target of $10.82. Bollinger theory says the price will continue in the trend until it has reached the opposite band. The theory also says that price action outside the Bollinger band implies more moves in the direction of the trend. The first day of price action outside the trend was on 15 August. The price continued higher, until a top of $10.92 on 20 August. The highest closing high occurred at $10.81 on 22 August, on a day when the price had gone back below the upper Bollinger band.

Stop-loss

The Bollinger band theory for a stop-loss level prescribes an exit at a close below the MA line. The price action did not close below the MA line until after it had hit the opposite Bollinger band and moved to the double-bottom target.

TRAILING STOP-LOSS LEVELS

Using a trailing stop involves moving your exit point as the price travels in the direction of the trend you are trading. This strategy is based on the theory 'a trend in motion will tend to stay in motion'.

As a new uptrend gains momentum, more and more buyers enter the market and take the price higher. Setting a trailing stop means you can catch the ride until the buyers start to diminish. As the uptrend progresses you can narrow the trailing stop-loss.

Most inexperienced traders enter a trade and tell themselves they are using something like a trailing stop. For example, how many of you made similar statements during the tech boom: 'Now that Solution 6 has reached $17, if it comes back, I won't get out lower than $15.' In reality, more small investors exited below $2 than anywhere near all-time highs.

Using a trailing stop means using a specific quantifiable formula rather than a vague level based on neat round numbers and wishful thinking. I have two favourite stop-loss methods. The first is a trailing stop based on Fibonacci levels, and the other uses support or resistance.

Fibonacci Trailing Stop-loss

A popular method to trail a stop-loss is to use a percentage based on the highs to lows of the trend. Being a Fibonacci enthusiast, I prefer the two key ratios 62 and 38 per cent. Because price tends to make bigger retracements at the beginning of a trend a 62 per cent retracement trailing stop is usually best as the rally sets sail. As the trend gains momentum, retracements tend to be smaller and a 38 per cent trailing stop can be used. This also means as your trade becomes more profitable, you are maximising your profits. It is surprising how often a stock will reverse at a 38 per cent level. Figure 6.5 (below) shows a theoretical model of a trailing stop calculated by using the Fibonacci 38 per cent level.

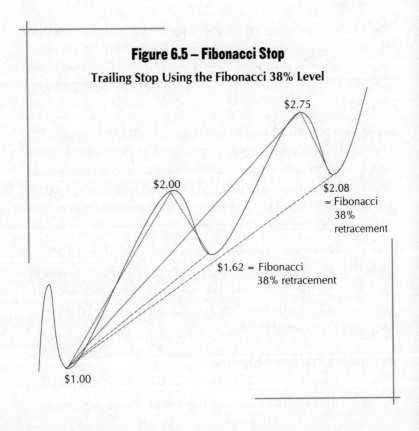

Figure 6.5 – Fibonacci Stop

Trailing Stop Using the Fibonacci 38% Level

$2.75

$2.00

$2.08
= Fibonacci
38%
retracement

$1.62 = Fibonacci
38% retracement

$1.00

A strong trend will have a minimal correction and the level of the retracement is frequently at or before this Fibonacci level. In fact, if a trending stock makes a retracement equal to or less than the Fibonacci 38 per cent level, then you can assume it will take out the previous trend extreme and continue to make even more gains in the direction of the trend.

A variation on the above system is a trailing Fibonacci 38 per cent where the starting point for each new Fibonacci calculation is moved up to the low of the most recent pullback. In the long trade example shown in Chart 6.8, the Fibonacci 38 per cent level could be based on the 30 October lows of $10.40 to the $12.31 highs, giving a level of $11.58. This would trigger an exit of the trade at the close of the day it gapped below this level (i.e. $11.52), or the open of the following day ($11.38).

The Fibonacci 38 per cent Stop and NCP

Chart 6.9 (overleaf) shows if you caught the rally in News Corp (NCP) that started on 10 October 2002, the first sign of correction occurred on 24 October. A high formed at $10.92 on 28 October. The low to use is the right leg of a double-bottom pattern at $8.57.

Overlaying the Fibonacci numbers gives a 38 per cent retracement level at $10.02. The actual low of the pullback was well above this at $10.40. The next high formed on the chart at $12.31. The Fibonacci 38 per cent retracement level based on the $8.57 low to the $12.31 high is $10.88. The price made lows of $10.82 and closed at $10.85 on 14 November before resuming the uptrend. Leaving a few cents distance between the Fibonacci level and the actual stop-loss level will ensure you are not stopped in this type of scenario.

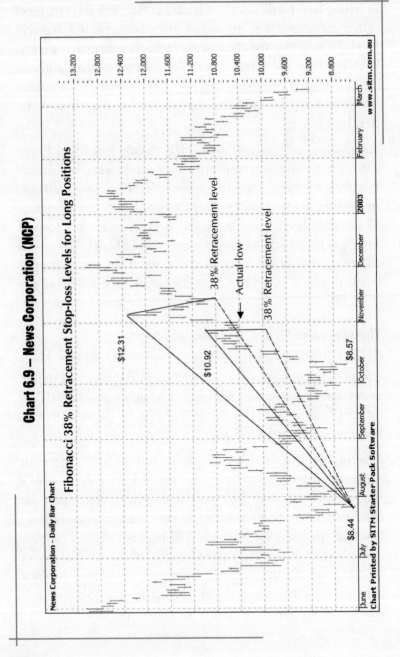

Chart 6.9 – News Corporation (NCP)

Fibonacci 38% Retracement Stop-loss Levels for Long Positions

News Corporation – Daily Bar Chart

Chart Printed by SITM Starter Pack Software

www.sitm.com.au

Trailing a Stop After a Gap

When gaps appear, the old rule is 'go with the gap'. This is especially true in a downtrend when the trend can accumulate steep momentum. Gaps left on the chart can be treated as potential areas of support and resistance.

A simple way to use a gap to trail your stop-loss level in a downtrend is to take the low of the day before the gap and place a stop-loss level a few cents above this level (see Figure 6.6, below). In an uptrend, work a stop just under the high of the day before the gap. The gap trailing stop-loss level method works best in the middle to late stages of a trend. A gap is less likely to be filled as the trend gathers momentum.

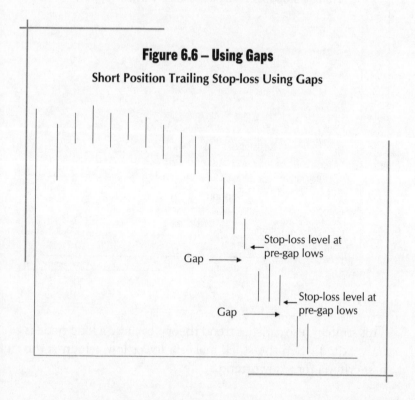

Figure 6.6 – Using Gaps

Short Position Trailing Stop-loss Using Gaps

The Support and Resistance Trailing Stop

A trailing stop can also be based on support or resistance. The idea that resistance becomes support and vice versa means that as the price breaks above resistance, this level should become support on a subsequent retracement. In a downtrend, a break below support should become resistance to further corrections to the upside. Thus, a stop can be trailed as each resistance or support point is breached in the direction of the trend (see Figure 6.7, below).

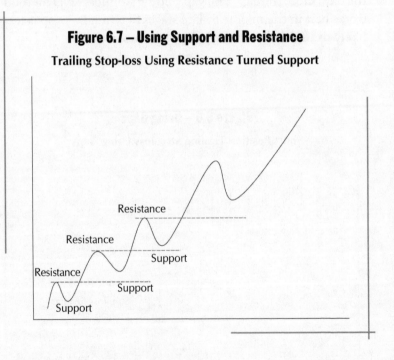

Figure 6.7 – Using Support and Resistance
Trailing Stop-loss Using Resistance Turned Support

This strategy also satisfies trend theory, because a long trade is only exited when the stock makes a lower low, which is the first criteria for a downtrend.

A variation of the support and resistance trailing stop is to use the second-to-last correction low as the basis for your stop-loss in an uptrend, and the second-to-last correction high in a downtrend (see Figure 6.8, below). Support or 'resistance turned' support can be used in an uptrend. In a downtrend resistance or 'support turned' resistance can become the basis for a stop-loss level.

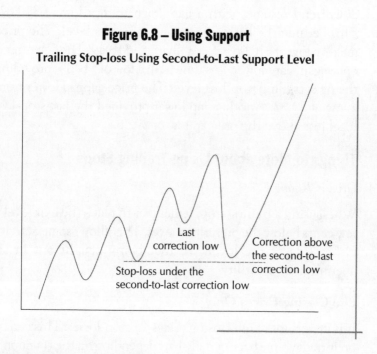

Figure 6.8 – Using Support

Trailing Stop-loss Using Second-to-Last Support Level

Last correction low

Correction above the second-to-last correction low

Stop-loss under the second-to-last correction low

Trailing Stop with NCP

Chart 6.10 (on page 123) shows that if you entered a short position somewhere near the top of the downtrend that started at $12.78 on 13 January you would have encountered the first rebound on 23 January. The first level of upside resistance is the low before the price gapped on 21 January. Therefore a stop-loss would have been placed just above $11.85. The next rebound occurred after the low of $11.06. The price rallied higher but could not close above the gap price of $11.51. The new stop-loss is now set at a few cents above $11.51.

The next rally on the chart goes to a high of $11.38 before making new lows at $10.58. A few cents above the $11.38 high is now the new trailing stop-loss level. The price gets to a high of $11.13 and once the price breaches the recent low, the stop-loss is moved down to a few cents above $11.13. The downtrend resumes with a gap down from a low of $10.82. This became the basis for the new stop-loss level. The price makes a low of $10.06 before rallying to $10.49. The downtrend once again gaps lower, this time from a low of $10.13, providing the next trailing stop-loss level. The price gapped lower from a low of $9.82. Another gap lower provided the last stop-loss level just above the pre-gap low of $9.56.

Things to Note about Using Trailing Stops

Give it Room

When using a trailing stop, remember to place the exit level a few cents below the prescribed level. This allows some activity either side of the level, without being caught out in an aberration of volatility.

Use Closing Prices Only

It is important to use closing prices for stop-losses. This can be on intraday time bars, or daily bars depending on the timeframe of your trading.

Back-test for Optimum Exit Method

Some stocks are better suited to different exit methods. For example a particularly volatile stock may continue in an uptrend but make larger retracements through the life of the uptrend.

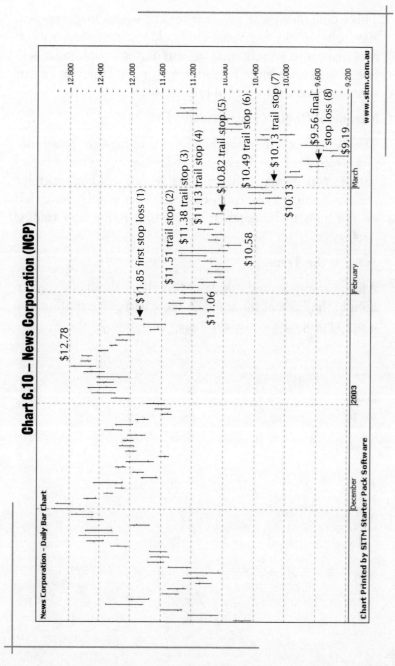

Chart 6.10 – News Corporation (NCP)

News Corporation – Daily Bar Chart

$12.78

$11.85 first stop loss (1)

$11.51 trail stop (2)

$11.38 trail stop (3)

$11.13 trail stop (4)

$11.06

$10.82 trail stop (5)

$10.58

$10.49 trail stop (6)

$10.13 trail stop (7)

$10.13

$9.56 final stop loss (8)

$9.19

Chart Printed by SITM Starter Pack Software

www.sitm.com.au

This would mean a 38 per cent trailing stop is inappropriate. Also some stocks do not adhere to old resistance levels when they make intermittent retracements during an uptrend. Back-test to match the right exit strategy (or combinations of exit strategies) for the historical price action.

Maximum Profit Versus Prudent Exit

The idea of a trailing stop-loss level is to preserve profit, not pick a top or bottom. Inexperienced traders never feel satisfied with a trade, no matter how profitable, unless it happens to be the exact point of reversal for a trend. Crying over money left on the table is the quickest way to undermine your trading strategy.

Stage of the Trend

All the stop-loss methods described above should be used in light of the stage of the trend. A more aggressive trailing stop is not appropriate at the early stage of a new trend.

chapter 7

CASE STUDY
NEWS CORPORATION (NCP)

Performing a market analysis is the first stage of a short-term trading approach. This should be a systematic process that results in a familiarity with the stock and the ability to accurately predict its potential for money-making opportunities with CFDs. To illustrate this process I will work through the example of a stock that is ideally suited to trade with CFDs. This analysis exercise could be your pro-forma for future analysis. When you perform your own version of this exercise for a stock, keep a record of this step-by-step process, because it will be the foundation of your trading approach and referred to during the trading process.

1. Long-term, Medium-term and Short-term Trend and Stage in the Trend

Long-Term

Bearish

Checking the monthly chart (see Chart 7.1, page 127), you can see NCP topped at $28 in March 2000 and embarked on a downtrend with the tech wreck that hit the market a month later. Since then, it has formed four major waves lower with the latest low at $8.44. This is around the chart low of $8.48 from October 1998 and the chart high of $8.42 of July 1995.

Medium-Term
Bullish

The monthy chart for NCP shows a good attempt to form a base at $8.44 (see Chart 7.1, opposite). There have been three subsequent tests and rejections of the $8.44 lows, including a series of two waves with higher highs. However, in the midst of a long-term downtrend, a multi-tested low that is eventually breached will usually travel a significant distance to the downside.

Short-Term
Range bound

After hitting a high of $13.02 in early December 2002, NCP made lows of $11.47 and rebounded to retest the highs (see Chart 7.2, page 128). A reversal pattern formed when the price rejected the $13.02 level, making it as high as $12.78, before closing below the $11.47 mark. The close below $11.47 was a short-term sell signal and the price duly fell. The price rallied, testing and rejecting the old chart support area of $11.47, proving the importance of this level for future resistance. The price eventually made lows at $9.19 before rebounding. On 21 March NCP hit a high of $11.42, once again rejected from the $11.47 highs to be rangebound between $11.42 and lows of $10.52.

Conclusion

From this analysis, the long-term outlook for NCP is bearish, but in the medium-term it may be forming a base. However the short-term horizon is range bound. From this I would conclude that NCP is in a mature downtrend, with the possibility of it being near the end of this trend or staging a medium-term rally.

Chart 7.1 – News Corporation (NCP) Monthly Chart

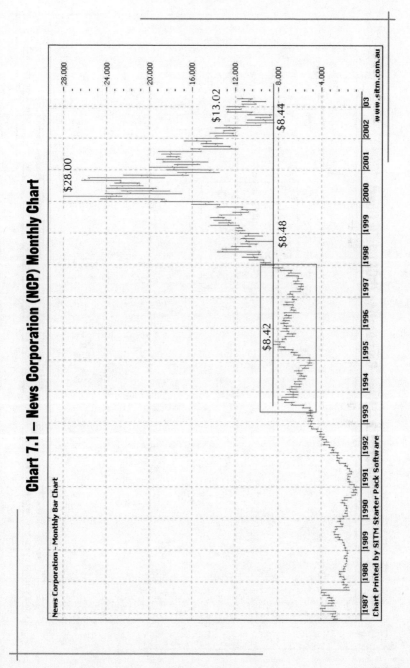

News Corporation – Monthly Bar Chart

Chart Printed by SITM Starter Pack Software

www.sitm.com.au

$28.00

$13.02

$8.48

$8.44

$8.42

Chart 7.2 – News Corporation (NCP) Daily Chart

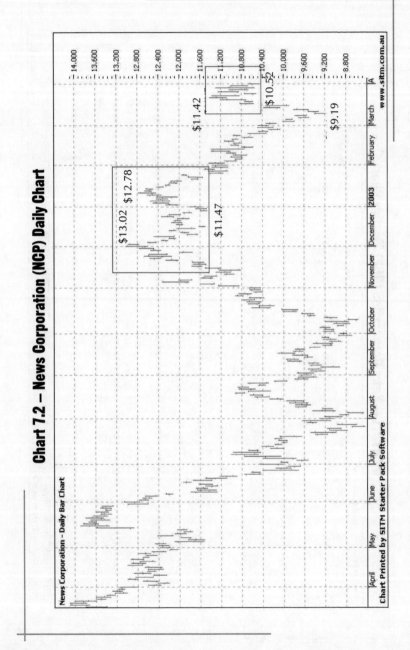

News Corporation - Daily Bar Chart

$13.02 $12.78

$11.47

$11.42

$10.52

$9.19

Chart Printed by SITM Starter Pack Software

www.sitm.com.au

However, a close below $8.44 would remove any chance of a reversal and change all horizons to negative.

2. Formation of Chart Patterns

Chart 7.3 (see page 131) of NCP shows a number of situations of an orderly consolidation pattern, where a breach of either side of the pattern on a closing basis causes a trend to develop in the direction of the break. However, there is a caveat to this. When NCP entered the initial phase of the downtrend after making the $13.02 high, it formed a consolidation range with a low of $11.50 reached on 16 December 2002. This was followed by a rally to a high of $12.34. On 30 December the price made lows at $11.47 but closed at $11.52. The next day it made lows at $11.47 and also closed at that level. The price closed below the original range low of $11.50 by 2¢, but then rallied back to test the upside.

This shows that, historically, NCP has given a false break-out signal by a few cents. Knowing that NCP has done this in the past means we should be aware of this possibly happening again. Therefore, a break of the current sideways pattern by a few cents should not necessarily be considered a definite trading signal.

Another important characteristic of the NCP chart is revealed when you study the past rallies that have occurred in the downtrend. These rallies have attempted and failed to result in a reversal of the downtrend, so they are important because they provide insight into how a potential reversal in the downtrend should not look. There have been two protracted consolidation patterns since the downtrend gained momentum in September 2000 (see Chart 7.4, page 132). The first occurred from December 2000 and gave way to new lows in September 2001. This potential bottoming pattern traded a range between a low of $13.51 and a high of $19.95. A second test of the downside was rejected at $14.75 in early April 2001. This was followed by two attempts to test the $19.95 level.

This two-wave action formed a set of higher lows but lower highs, the first clue that the potential reversal would not follow through to the upside.

The next failed potential reversal occurred from the September 2001 low of $11.78. Over the next five months, NCP traded up to around the halfway mark of the previous rally, before making lows at $11.82 in February 2002. The low of $11.82 was breached on a closing basis in May 2002, but was followed by a strong rebound. However the rally could not exceed the previous rally high and the price resumed the downtrend to make new lows.

3. Daily and Weekly Ranges

The end of a downtrend is characterised by diminishing ranges. If the current price action for NCP is a bottom, then it should be displaying less volatility.

Without performing specific calculations it is obvious that the current rally is trading in similar ranges to previous failed bounces in the downtrend. The previous rally for NCP was launched from a congestion pattern that lasted nearly five years from 1993 until late 1997. This is highlighted in Chart 7.1. Note the presence of low range waves with little upside progress. After such a protracted and dramatic downtrend as the recent correction, you might expect NCP to spend a number of years trading sideways before it enters a new sustainable uptrend. Anything less should probably be considered a dead cat bounce.

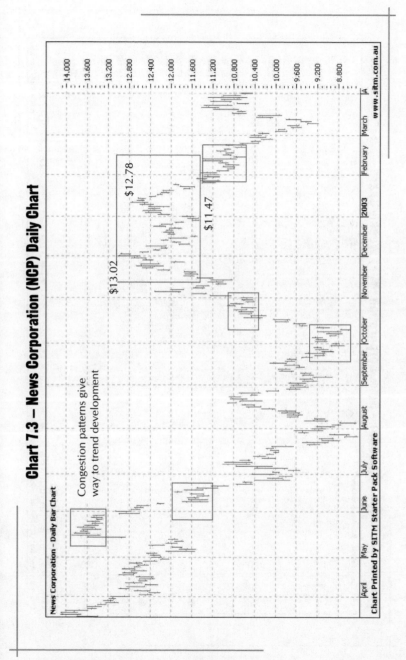

Chart 7.3 – News Corporation (NCP) Daily Chart

News Corporation – Daily Bar Chart

Congestion patterns give way to trend development

$13.02

$12.78

$11.47

Chart Printed by SITM Starter Pack Software

www.sitm.com.au

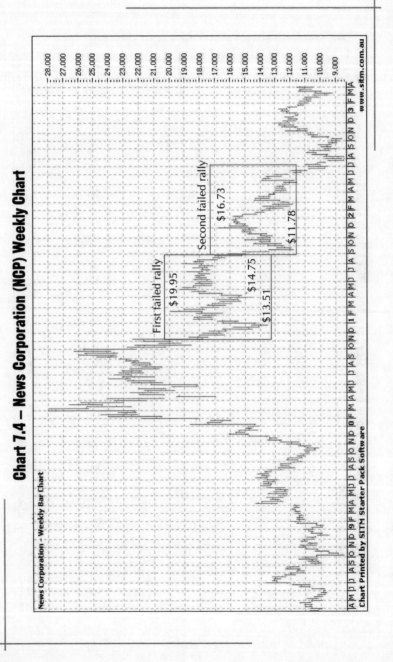

Chart 7.4 – News Corporation (NCP) Weekly Chart

News Corporation - Weekly Bar Chart

Chart Printed by SITM Starter Pack Software

www.sitm.com.au

First failed rally
$19.95
$14.75
$13.51

Second failed rally
$16.73
$11.78

4. Previous Support and Resistance and Retracement Levels

The idea of previous support becoming resistance and vice versa occurs frequently on the NCP chart (see Chart 7.5, overleaf). Resistance at $10.92 was first encountered in August 2002. Another test and rejection of this level occurred in October 2002. Once this level was breached, it became support for a pull back in November 2002. New highs at $13.02 were followed by lows at $11.47. This level was retested as resistance in January, February and March 2003. Calculating the Fibonacci level based on the highs and lows of the downtrend to date reveals the $13.02 level coincides with the Fibonacci 23.6 per cent level (see Chart 7.6, page 135). This adds extra significance to the resistance level. The next important Fibonacci level is the 38.2 per cent level which is at $15.91.

Key Points About NCP

↳ NCP could be considered in a long-term downtrend, with a medium-term bottom forming on the chart. The medium-term bottom fails at a close below $8.44. The short-term outlook is rangebound but turns to bullish at a close above $11.42 to $11.47 and bearish at a close below $10.52.

↳ Current price action (April 2003) is looking similar to failed bottoming patterns. Beware of false break-outs to the downside.

↳ Expect good trending activity when a congestion pattern is breached on a closing basis.

↳ High volatility in daily and weekly ranges indicates the downtrend is not near an end.

↳ Previous resistance to watch: $11.47–$11.52; $12.78; $13.02. Previous support to watch: $10.52–$10.46; $8.44.

↳ Key resistance levels ahead: $11.42; $11.56.

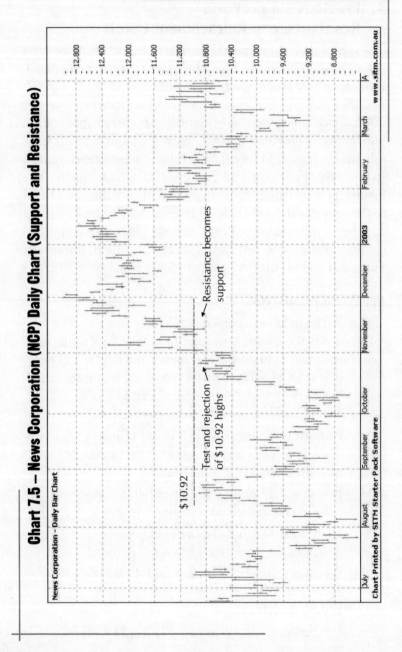

Chart 7.5 – News Corporation (NCP) Daily Chart (Support and Resistance)

News Corporation – Daily Bar Chart

$10.92

Test and rejection of $10.92 highs

Resistance becomes support

Chart Printed by SITM Starter Pack Software

www.sitm.com.au

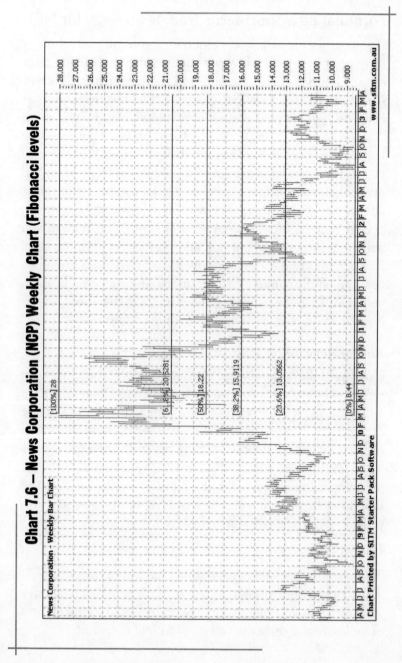

Chart 7.6 – News Corporation (NCP) Weekly Chart (Fibonacci levels)

News Corporation – Weekly Bar Chart

[100%] 28

[61.8%] 20.5281

[50%] 18.22

[38.2%] 15.9119

[23.6%] 13.0562

[0%] 8.44

Chart Printed by SITM Starter Pack Software

www.sitm.com.au

Formulating a Short-term Trading Strategy for NCP

If you opt for life as a short-term trader, you can trade short or long positions with CFDs without regard to the long-term trend. However, it is far easier from a psychological perspective to sell when the general outlook is bearish. The rebounds that occur in a downtrend can be unpredictable and much more difficult to trade. Upside targets, based on chart patterns, are less likely to work in a downtrend than an uptrend. The reverse is also true. Therefore, selling from double tops or other top reversal patterns is more likely to yield a move to your target area swiftly with little retracement in a downtrend. However, as you become more experienced at short-term trading you will be able to switch outlook and positions with more ease. Some traders find they instinctively prefer a bearish or bullish position on the market. If you're underlying outlook is bearish, you may find you always prefer to take the short trades notwithstanding the general prevailing conditions.

Buy Strategy for NCP

On 1 April the price rebounded from the lows of the congestion range and gave a short-term buy signal (see Chart 7.7, page 138). It is likely NCP will continue higher and test the upside of the range. A close above the high of the congestion pattern of $11.42 would be the cue for more buyers to enter the market and should send the stock even higher. However, other resistance, including the $11.47 previous support and the Fibonacci 62 per cent retracement level of $11.56 could also provide some barrier to further gains.

Entry Point

There are two possible entry points for a long trade in NCP. The first is more aggressive—buy at the open of the next day's trade. The more prudent long position would be taken at a close above the resistance range of $11.42 to $11.56.

Profit Target

The first target for the buy on open trade would be the upper range of the congestion pattern. If you thought the uptrend looked set to continue, then you would narrow your trailing stop-loss and protect your profits while gaining exposure to further gains.

The first target on a close above congestion trade is the vertical distance of that congestion pattern added to the high of that pattern (a target at $12.32).

Stop-loss

A close below the low of 1 April at $10.45 would be the trigger for more selling and, therefore, a stop-loss a few cents below this level would be a safe exit for the buy on open trade. For the buy above resistance trade, place a stop-loss level just below the last low of the rally that takes the price to the break-out point. This is not known until the price reaches the entry point.

Sell Strategy for NCP

Since March 18, NCP formed a range on Chart 7.7 (see overleaf) between $11.42 and $10.52. The downside of this 90¢ range was tested and rejected on 1 April when the price fell to a low of $10.45 and closed at $10.63. This was a bullish signal and indicated it will likely test the upside the following day, and may rally for a further day or two in the manner of the rally of 10–12 February and the rallies of 2–6 January and 9–13 January. A classic reversal signal for this rally would be a higher open and test of the $11.42 range, with a close low in the daily range and a rejection of that level. If this occurred, it would represent an exhaustion of buying pressure and NCP will likely retest the $10.52 level again.

Having established a possible shorting set-up the next thing to do is establish specific parameters for this trade.

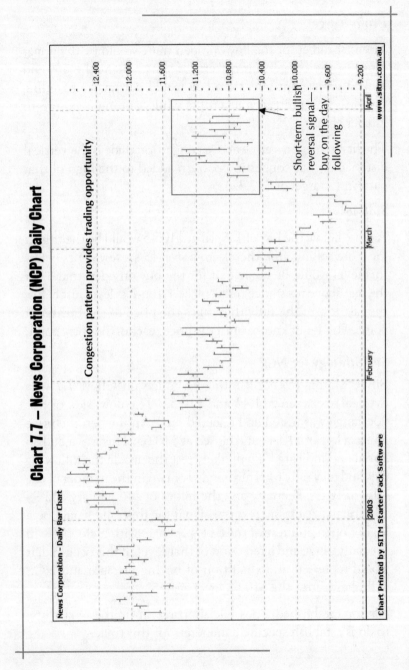

Chart 7.7 – News Corporation (NCP) Daily Chart

News Corporation - Daily Bar Chart

Congestion pattern provides trading opportunity

Short-term bullish reversal signal—buy on the day following

Chart Printed by SITM Starter Pack Software

www.sitm.com.au

Entry Point

The short position would be initiated at a break of the downside congestion range, which is now at $10.45. False break-out is unlikely since this will represent the third test of the support level of $10.52. Past data suggests this may happen on a gap.

Profit Target

The first downside target is found by measuring the vertical distance of the pattern and deducting it from the break-out point. Based on the $11.42 high to the $10.52 low the first target for NCP would be $9.62. However, another sell-off in the downtrend after two unsuccessful attempts to go higher is likely to send the stock much lower. After the initial break of support, a series of gapping moves could develop. This would require a more aggressive trailing stop, based on the recent high of preceding the gap.

Stop-loss

If the sell signal occurs after a gap, then the stop-loss can be placed at a few cents above the high of the day preceding the gap. Trail the stop-loss to use the most recent rebound high or the high of the day preceding a gap.

Conclusions

There are two important features of the strategy for NCP. Firstly, there is an upside and downside trade. Secondly, both require the right set-up of events before entering. With a strategy in place the investor stalks the market and waits for the price to create the correct circumstances as per the analysis. The hard part is fighting the urge to buy or sell as soon as it looks likely to break a particular level without it actually happening. Opening prices are notoriously misleading of the day's activity and can trap many short-term traders who jump in prematurely. Where a market closes is the definitive representation of the day's sentiment.

OTHER TRADING
STRATEGIES

INDEX TRADING

Taking advantage of a move in the value of a stock market index was previously only possible using a futures contract. Futures trading involves a standardised instrument as well as the payment of brokerage and GST to enter and exit a trade. Index CFD trading allows you to skip the brokerage and GST, and also, despite first appearances, benefit from an improved overall spread.

CFD providers generally offer CFDs on all major global stock market indices. Index CFDs are given names similar to the official names of the exchange index.

The price quoted by your CFD provider is generally based on the price of the equivalent futures contract, less the fair value. The spread is then formed by deducting and adding one point to either side of the new index level.

Scenario

Let's say you believe the Australian stock market will fall and you decide to sell an index CFD. The S&P/ASX 200 index is quoted by the Australian Stock Exchange (ASX) at 2939.

Your CFD provider quotes the price of the Aussie 200 at 2938–2940. Unlike a futures contract, where the point value of the trade is fixed to $25, you nominate the point value at which you want to trade. You then pay a deposit based on the point value assigned to the trade multiplied by 1 per cent.

For a $25 point value this would be:

$$25 \times 2938 \times 1\% = \$733.75$$

After one week, the index has fallen by 100 points. You then buy back at the offer price of 2839, after seeing a quote on the S&P/ASX 200 for 2838. The total profit on the position is calculated as:

$$2938 - 2839 = 99$$
$$99 \times \$25 = \$2,475$$

You must also take into account any cost or benefit from rolling over your index CFD position each day. Your position is rolled over by the difference in daily fair value for your index. (More detail on fair value and CFD index pricing is found in Chapter 2—'Frequently Asked Questions'.)

Compared to Futures

A short position is opened through your futures broker at the bid price of 2939. You pay brokerage of around $25 plus GST of $2.50. A deposit of $3,000 is deducted from your account. Total funds required to open the position is $3,027.50. A week later you close the position. The quote on the exchange is 2838–2839. You buy at 2839 and your profit is calculated as 100 x 25 = $2,500, less brokerage and GST to enter and exit the trade which equals a total of $55.00.

Net proceeds are $2,445.

SECTOR TRADING

Investing in the stock market is supposedly 80 per cent market or sector risk and only 20 per cent company specific. This means it is four times more important to choose the right sector than the right stock. Some CFD providers allow you to take a position on sectors. The sectors available to trade are based on the international GICS categories (for more information on the GICS sectors, go to the ASX website—www.asx.com.au). For instance, dealforforee.com offers ten sector CFDs. They are Consumer Discretionary, Consumer Staple, Energy, Financial, Health, Industrial, Information Technology, Materials, Telecoms and Utilities.

Scenario

Let's say you believe the financial sector has topped out and will fall from current levels.

The last quoted price on the ASX for the Financial index is 3887.2. Your CFD provider is quoting a spread of 3885–3889. You sell five Financial index CFDs at 3885, which means each one point move in the sector index will cause a $5 move in the value of your position. Your are required to pay a deposit of 1 per cent of the total value, calculated as:

$$3885 \times \$5 \times 1\% = \$194.25$$

In a month's time the Financial sector index has fallen 50 points to 3837. Your CFD provider is quoting a spread on the Financial index CFD at 3835–3839. You decide to close your position by buying at the offer of 3839. The result is calculated as follows:

$$3885 - 3839 = 46 \text{ points}$$
$$46 \times \$5 = \$230$$

In addition you may receive rollover benefit which takes into account interest and dividend expectations (see Chapter 2—'Frequently Asked Questions').

HEDGING A SINGLE STOCK

If you have a single shareholding that looks set to fall in value, it is possible to offset potential losses without selling the stock. The process of recouping losses in your physical shareholding by profiting from a secondary or derivative instrument is known as hedging. Hedging a single stock with a CFD is a popular tool with investors who have been remunerated with stock and options from their employers. If you are invested in a business that is undergoing a short- to medium-term downturn, taking a short position in the CFD market locks-in profits and offsets further losses.

Scenario

You bought 10,000 Lihir Gold Limited (LHG) shares at $1.00 a year ago. The shares have done well and now trade at $1.32, but you are worried the price will fall in the short-term with a correction in the gold price.

To combat this, you sell 10,000 CFDs on Lihir at the bid price of $1.32. You pay a margin deposit of 5 per cent of the underlying value calculated as follows:

$$10,000 \times \$1.32 \times 5\% = \$660$$

Three months later LHG is trading at $1.20. You believe LHG has bottomed and want to lift the hedge by buying back the CFD on LHG.

Your physical share position is down $1,200 in value, but this is unrealised and remains a 'paper' loss. The price quoted by your CFD provider is $1.20. The return from your short position is calculated as :

$$1.32 - 1.20 = 12¢$$
$$11¢ \times 10,000 = \$1,200$$

You will also receive interest from your short CFD position, which is calculated approximately:

$$10,000 \times 1.32 \times 3.25\% \times 90/365 = \$105.78$$

HEDGING A PORTFOLIO OF STOCKS

In the last few years the spectre of a bear market has loomed large. Yet many investors are loathe to part with shareholdings they have built up over a period of years and are still showing a good profit. An alternative to exiting the market altogether is to hedge using an index CFD.

Scenario

Let's say you inherit a $1 million portfolio of blue chip stocks that has undergone a significant capital gain since it was established. The stock market is looking weak and you do not wish to lose money from a potential bear market. At the same time, selling now would mean a large tax bill.

You decide to sell an Aussie 200 index CFD to hedge your newly acquired share portfolio. This means any losses in the physical holding will be offset by gains in your CFD position and vice versa. The last traded price for the Aussie 200 index is 2938. To determine the dollar value of the CFD index you wish to sell, divide the total value of your portfolio by the current value of the index— $1 million divided by 2938. This gives a value of 340.37, which means your order will be to sell the Aussie 200 for $340 per point.

To open the position you are required to pay a deposit margin of 1 per cent of the underlying value, which is calculated as:

$$1\% \times 2{,}938 \times \$340 = \$9{,}989.20$$

Compared to Futures

Each contract has a value of $25 per point. You determine the number of contracts it will take to cover your portfolio of stocks by multiplying the value of the index by $25. Multiplying $25 by 2938 equals $73,450. Divide $1 million by $73,450 to get a contract number of 13.6147. Choosing 14 futures contracts will overhedge your exposure and 13 contracts will underhedge your exposure. The amount underhedged is 0.6 of a future:

$$0.6 \times \$25 = \$15$$

If underhedged there is a shortfall in the hedge of $15 per index point move. On a 150 point move of the index this totals $2,250. The cost of trading 14 futures contracts is around $25 per contract plus GST, which is $350 plus $35.

PAIRS TRADING

How does the performance of your stock compare to a key stock in the sector, the sector as a whole, or the index? An analysis of the relative performance of a stock highlights opportunities to make money on this differential. This is known as pairs trading.

AMP Comparisons

You can gauge a lot about a share by placing its price action in a context. I first became interested in the idea of comparative performance when I reviewed the price action of AMP around the September 11, 2001 disaster. My first comparison was with the general market index—S&P/ASX 200.

September 11, 2001

The S&P/ASX200 index topped in June and July 2001 at 3490. The World Trade Center disaster sent the index from a closing price on September 11, 2001 at 3242 to a low of 2882 on September 24. This was a drop of 11 per cent. The total loss from the June/July highs to the September lows was 17 per cent. AMP on the other hand closed on September 11 at $19.02. On September 19 it made lows at $16.35, a fall of 14 per cent from its pre-disaster close.

More interesting perhaps is a comparison of AMP's fall from its highs of June 2000. At this time AMP was trading at $22 and the stock market index was making all-time highs. The percentage loss from these highs to the September lows was nearly 26 per cent, this compares to a 17 per cent drop for the index.

Post September 11, 2001

Following the shock of September 11, 2001, the market rallied across the board. The S&P/ASX 200 retested the highs making new all-time highs at 3506 in February 2002. While the general stock market roared back to its pre-disaster levels, AMP limped higher, but then lost steam around April 2002. By June 2002, it was trading below its September 2001 lows. This means in June last year investors were more negative about AMP than when the disaster struck, and this was well before the bad news about it UK operations had come to light. AMP's performance relative to the rest of the insurance sector was also giving early warning signs about its future performance.

While the whole sector took a dive after the September 11 disaster, the share price for AMP has consistently underperformed relative to the sector since the event. When AMP closed below its September 2001 lows, it was the first company in the sector to do so.

Checking the relative performance of the other key players in the sector gives an insight. These companies include AXA Asia Pacific Holdings Limited (AXA), Suncorp Metway

Limited (SUN), Insurance Australia Group Limited (IAG) and QBE Insurance Group Limited (QBE).

QBE is now in a new uptrend and continues to gain ground. IAG tested and fell below its September 2001 lows in October 2002, but is now trading 12 per cent above this. SUN fell below its September lows in February 2003, although is now (April 2003) trading 25¢ above those levels. AXA closed below its September lows in March 2003 and is now (April 2003) a few cents above that level.

Banking Sector Comparisons

AMP was the worst performer of the insurance sector, even before the bad news hit the market, and well before it breached its all-time low. Which stock has been underperforming in the banking sector? Using the September 11, 2001 event as a yardstick, it probably won't be a surprise to know that Commonwealth Bank of Australia Limited (CBA) has been the worst performer. It is the only stock of the big four—NAB, CBA, ANZ and WBC—to cross below this benchmark and had lost 34 per cent in value by March 14, 2003. This is how the other three have travelled:

↳ National Australia Bank Limited (NAB) rebounded at the Fibonacci 62 per cent level, measuring from its September 2001 lows to its all-time highs. This was a 28 per cent loss in value from its all-time highs, and within 20 per cent of the September 2001 lows. The current rally in global markets has seen the value of NAB rise 16 per cent from its recent March lows. In April 2003, NAB is around 10 per cent away from all-time highs.

↳ Westpac Banking Corporation Limited (WBC) fell to within 9 per cent of its September 2001 lows and a total of 24.5 per cent from its highs in February 2003. But a rebound since this has sent WBC within 8 per cent of the old highs. A new uptrend for WBC is not confirmed until it closes above the all-time highs.

↳   ANZ Banking Group Limited (ANZ) lost nearly 24 per cent of its value from the all-time highs when it fell to lows in late February 2003, and this was 18 per cent away from its September 2001 lows. It is now (April 2003) 12 per cent away from these highs and, like the rest of the sector, currently in the midst of a sharp rally.

Don't Bank on It

There is another context in which all of this needs to be considered, and that is the price before the 'war rally' (Iraq 2003) in global financial markets. The stock market was already in a confirmed downtrend before it occurred. Certainly, this rally is not the kind of rebound we saw in 1997 or 1998, where the prices took a sharp fall and an equally swift recovery to resume the uptrend. Markets had made significant losses in terms of not just price but also time, having been heading south for around a year.

The September 2001 lows continue to be a benchmark of underlying strength and I consider the most important barometer of a stock's health to be its downside performance relative to this level. This doesn't change my perception for the outlook for CBA as the next biggest loser in the playground. However, it does take some of the shine off WBC, which has been increasingly heralded as the star of the sector. After CBA, it is the next worst banking stock in terms of the distance to test the September lows, trading within 8 per cent of that level. ANZ was 18 per cent away and NAB was 20 per cent.

Pairs Trading with Stocks

A pairs trade is known as a spread trade in futures markets and means the simultaneous buying and selling of different stocks, or a stock and an index or sector CFD to take advantage of a relative move in price.

Scenario

Let's say you think CBA will continue to underperform in relation to the Financials sector. You therefore sell share CFDs on CBA and buy a Financial index CFD. CBA is trading around $27 and is quoted by the CFD provider at $27.00–$27.01. The Financial sector was last quoted at 3895 on the ASX and a spread of 3893–3897 by the CFD provider. To determine the relative amount of CBA to trade to the sector index, divide the index level by the mid-price of CBA:

$$3895 / 27.00 = 144.26$$

You buy the Financial sector CFD for $5 per point (which means multiplying the amount of CBA share CFDs by 5) at the current offer of 3897, pay a deposit of 1 per cent and simultaneously sell a CFD on CBA at the bid price of $27.00, paying a 5 per cent deposit:

$$\$5 \times 3897 \times 1\% = \$194.85$$
$$(144 \times 5) \times \$27.00 \times 5\% = \$972.00$$

Total deposit required is:

$$\$194.85 + 972.00 = \$1,166.85$$

In a month's time the index has fallen to a value of 3845 and CBA is trading at $24.89. Your positions are closed at the current spread on the index at 3843–3847 and CBA is quoted at $24.89–$24.90.

The index position is calculated as:

$$3897 - 3843 = 54 \text{ points}$$
$$52 \times 5 = \$270 \text{ loss}$$

The share CFD profit is calculated as:

$$\$27.00 - \$24.90 = \$2.10$$
$$721 \times \$2.10 = \$1514.10 \text{ profit}$$

The result is $1,514 less $270, which equals $1,244. (Note that interest receipts would also be added to the profits.)

A pairs trade for CBA could also be initiated against NAB or even the general market index. Pairs trading is profitable as long as the relative move between the two CFDs widens. A profitable pairs trade is not contingent on the direction of the market. The above scenario would have been profitable if both the CBA and the financial sector rallied, as long as CBA did not rally as strongly as the sector CFD.

BUY AND HOLD

CFDs are usually associated with short-term trading. However, a CFD buy-and-hold strategy can be a very effective way to participate in a bull market. A buy and hold CFD strategy offers several advantages over the other types of leveraged exposure to the sharemarket, such as margin lending.

When you purchase shares in a traditional way you pay the entire cost of the shares upfront. CFD trading means you are buying and paying a percentage, usually only 5 to 10 per cent of the underlying value. That gives you 90 to 95 per cent of your capital to put elsewhere. You can effectively have exposure to $100,000 of shares with just $5,000 of capital used as deposit.

When using a long-term buy and hold strategy with CFDs, only take a position with an underlying value that is within your current means. The beauty of a buy and hold strategy is the ability to enter the market and not worry about short-term falls in price. Because of the leverage factor, if you trade a CFD position that is uncomfortably large in underlying terms, each movement downwards will create anxiety and possibly push you out of your long-term strategy. Buy and hold strategies are meant to weather the short-term storms of a bull market. Only trade in CFD positions with an underlying size you can afford.

Opposite is a comparison between a buy-and-hold strategy using:

↳ $100,000 with outright shareholding
↳ a margin loan with $100,000 underlying
↳ a CFD position with $100,000 underlying.

Sell and Hold

If buy and hold was the mantra of the 1990s then it is inevitable that at some time the cyclical nature of financial markets means the Zeitgeist will be 'sell and hold'. When stocks such a Telstra, Lend Lease and AMP suffer major corrections and go from blue blood status to distinctly doggy, then you know the stock market is on shaky ground. Even if your macro view is not bearish, CFDs make it possible to jump on board the likes of the next AMP in the early stages and ride the trend all the way down. Here is a how a sell and hold strategy might have worked for AMP.

Buy Shares Outright
- ↳ Cost of shares $100,000
- ↳ Add cost of brokerage
- ↳ Outlay $100,000 plus brokerage.

Margin Loan
- ↳ Pay deposit to broker of 20 per cent or $20,000
- ↳ Client receives $80,000 to buy shares
- ↳ Repays loan of $80,000 at rate of RBA overnight cash rate plus around 3.0 to 5.0 per cent (in April 2003 approximately 7.5 per cent), which equals $6,000
- ↳ Pay brokerage for share transactions
- ↳ Total outlay $20,000 plus interest cost of $2,200 ($6,000 – $3,800) plus brokerage (where $3,800 is the interest received on the $80,000 invested at overnight rate of 4.75 per cent).

Buy and Hold CFDs
- ↳ Pay deposit of $5,000
- ↳ Pay interest on total exposure at rate of RBA overnight rate plus 1 per cent (5.75 per cent at the time of writing) on $100,000—equals $5,750
- ↳ No brokerage fees
- ↳ Receive interest on balance of $95,000 deposited at bank at 4.75 per cent— equals approximately $4,500
- ↳ Total outlay $5,000 plus interest cost of $1,250 ($5,750 – $4,500).

Note that this comparison does not take into account variation margin or dividend receipts.

Assumes capital not used to trade is invested and receives interest at the overnight cash rate.

Scenario

AMP makes new all-time lows by closing below $13.58 on 5 August 2002 (see Chart 8.1, opposite). You believe this is a significant bearish signal and wait for a rebound before shorting 1,000 AMP CFDs. The following day the price of AMP opens at $13.01. A day later the price rallies and eventually hits a high of $14.78 on 20 August. From there it forms a low of $13.90 and then retests the $14.78 highs. Failing to follow through to the upside, you sell on a close below the $13.90 support level. This gets you short on the open of the following day at $13.67, with a stop-loss above the recent highs of $14.78. You are short for the long-term (see Chart 8.2, page 156).

The margin deposit is calculated as:

$$\$13.67 \times 1,000 \times 5\% = \$683.50$$

As at 14 April 2003, AMP was trading at $7.36. This represented a profit of $6.31 per share or a total of $6,310. Profit on this position would be enhanced by the financing amount—based on the current interest rate—on the underlying value of the position that would be paid to your account for the duration of the sell and hold trade.

Chart 8.1 – AMP Limited (AMP) Weekly Chart

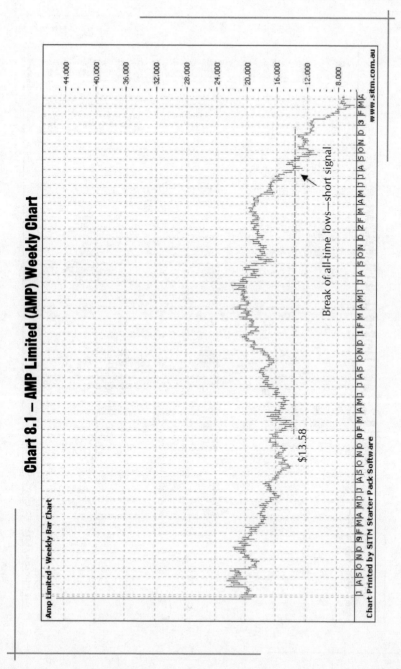

Amp Limited – Weekly Bar Chart

$13.58

Break of all-time lows—short signal

Chart Printed by SITM Starter Pack Software

www.sitm.com.au

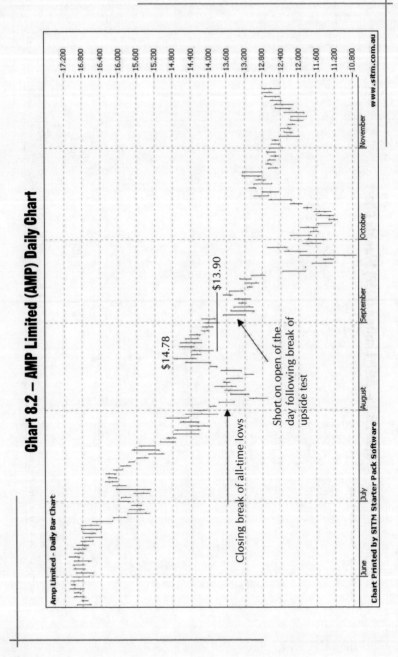

Chart 8.2 – AMP Limited (AMP) Daily Chart

Amp Limited – Daily Bar Chart

$14.78

$13.90

Closing break of all-time lows

Short on open of the day following break of upside test

Chart Printed by SITM Starter Pack Software

www.sitm.com.au

chapter 9

MONEY MANAGEMENT AND PSYCHOLOGY

MANAGING LOSSES

CFDs Versus Share Trading

If you are an experienced share trader, you will find one of the biggest differences between CFDs and traditional share trading is the management of losses. Consider the comparison of buying shares and buying CFDs:

You buy Telstra at $5.00 and it drops to $4.00. Your shareholding of 1,000 TLS shares means the value of the holding has now decreased in value by $1,000. But unless you sell your shares at this lower value, the loss does not directly affect you.

On the other hand, a CFD trader with a long position of 1,000 share CFDs will have $1,000 deducted from his or her account if the price of Telstra drops from $5.00 to $4.00.

Just reading about this fact doesn't leave much impact, but when you trade CFDs and actually experience a deduction from your account it creates a very different psychology of loss.

When every price move in the wrong direction causes you to lose money and that result is obvious and material, you will find the trading process more stressful. Stress and pain in trading can motivate you to take chances, lose sight of your initial trading strategy and take the enjoyment out of the trading process.

Loss Causes Inertia

The question you will probably ask yourself when you first experience a loss on your CFD account is, 'why didn't I exit that losing trade as soon as I realised I was wrong?' Another question you might ask is, 'why did I spend so much time making the decision to exit the trade when I can enter a trade without much thought at all?'

Losing trades can bring on a kind of inertia. Understanding the process of loss via the charts can help you avoid it.

Attachment to the Trend

When we are long, the higher a price goes, the more attachment we form to the trade. If we don't have a specific trading strategy and the price meanders higher, with frequent pauses and retracements, we are more likely to jump ship sooner rather than later. Ironically, the fast-moving uptrend is far more vulnerable to a rapid and large correction, and the less likely we are to cut the position when it pulls back. It is these large and rapid corrections that frighten us into a state of inactivity.

It is this inertia that can cause us to lose money. We might have had the best intentions of exiting at the first sign of trouble but when the big hit happens, we become inert and unable to pull the trigger.

Telstra and Managing Losses

Many Australians own Telstra and continue to hold, despite the reversal that started in February 1999. Applying a couple of basic technical analysis tools would have shown a clear end to the party. A simple trendline drawn from the mid-1998 lows showed a decisive break around a year later. While the price stayed rangebound between a $9.20 high and the $7.31 low, TLS showed the possibility of closing above the highs and going even higher. However, as soon as it closed below the range, the uptrend was over because the stock had confirmed a triple top pattern.

In March 2000, directly following the breach of support, TLS had a rally that spiked at $8.78. The spike represented high emotional involvement and was a clear indication that market participants were acting with more desperation than sense (see Chart 9.1, overleaf).

The Bear Market Trap

A spurt of strong buying often follows a break of major support during a downtrend. It is more common early on in downtrends and feeds off investor's hope. When investors see their favourite blue chip suffer some profit-taking, they may consider exiting the stock. But, while they are in the process of making up their minds to exit, the price snaps back.

This kind of rapid reaction is known as the dead cat bounce (discussed earlier). Smart traders know the significance of the break, but many amateurs are still locked into a buy-low–sell-high mentality and see the new lows as an opportunity to pick up stock cheaply. When the stock rises rapidly as a consequence, their faith is renewed and they stay hopeful of a complete turnaround.

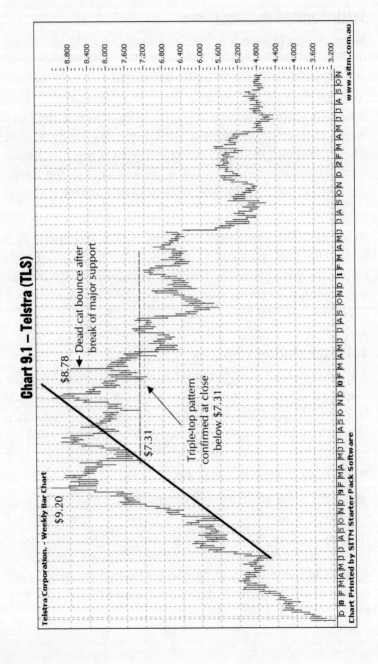

Chart 9.1 – Telstra (TLS)

Telstra Corporation. – Weekly Bar Chart

$9.20

$8.78

← Dead cat bounce after break of major support

$7.31

Triple-top pattern confirmed at close below $7.31

Chart Printed by SITM Starter Pack Software

www.sitm.com.au

Exiting on the Reaction

The obvious approach to this scenario is to try to exit a long position on the reaction, or dead cat bounce. This is tempting, but very tricky. Watching a stock rally after you have exited at a break of major support can be disheartening, but not as painful as watching it make new lows.

I suspect there were many TLS shareholders wishing they had sold at $7.20, despite the subsequent rally to $8.78—especially in light of the April 2003 price that is somewhere round the $4.00 range. Your priority should be to have a strategy that removes any emotional attachment in your trading decisions. Waiting for a dead cat bounce to exit is a sure way to become victim to your emotional swings. Disciplined traders use a predetermined stop-loss level, rather than waiting optimistically for a dead cat bounce.

STOP-LOSS AND MONEY MANAGEMENT

A stock will generally give you more than one opportunity to exit comfortably at relatively high levels. In the case of TLS, the first sign was around $8.00 in 1999. The second indicated exit was around $7.30 in October of that year. Keep in mind, the aim of the game is to make money with minimum stress— not to pick tops.

It is important to prepare for the change in emotion that surrounds trading a leverage product. Take advantage of the flexibility of CFDs, but only take positions that sit well with your comfort level.

There are two factors that affect the placement of your stop-loss —previous price action on the chart and your appetite for risk. These two factors are the foundation of your money management policy.

The Percentage Stop-loss

Basing your exit on a percentage of capital is, in my opinion, a frustrating and illogical approach. This is because the markets don't know or care how much money you can afford to lose. Therefore, any stop-loss that is not based on historical price action suggests that your trading strategy is really no better than throwing a dart at the chart.

My 'Ideal' Stop-loss

The ideal stop-loss strategy is a combination of chart analysis and risk comfort. It is a process of weighing up the level at which the trade might fail against the amount of money this possibility would involve. Moreover, if a trade you wish to take involves risking a greater percentage of capital than you would be prepared to lose, then you shouldn't take the trade. This doesn't mean taking the trade with a tighter stop-loss or trading with your fingers crossed. It simply means not taking the trade.

There will be many trades in your trading career that will fit your criteria. Never feel compelled to take a trade, no matter how attractive it looks. Remember, all trades look like the jackpot before you enter.

If you follow the above approach, then your stop-loss is determined before you take the trade. This is a crucial element of success. Knowing exactly when your trade will fail is easier beforehand and obvious in hindsight, but it can become a very grey area when you are in the middle of a losing trade. This is because losing money makes us irrational and desperate.

Treat it Like a Business

Dan Gramza, an American candlestick expert, used the analogy of owning a shop when describing trading. Sometimes you buy stock that doesn't sell. This is a mistake, you take a loss, and you don't buy the same stock again. Using the same objective approach will help you stick to your rules.

PSYCHOLOGY OF WINNING AND LOSING

Trading is like Surfing

There is a famous expression, used by whimsical old surfers, that goes something like this: 'when you understand the sea, you understand life.' Recently, I have been learning to surf, but in the process spent much more time trying not to inadvertently steal a wave from a seething teenager than grasp the deeper meaning of the experience. However, being a bit of a 'chart nut', I think the expression could be borrowed and applied with equal sagacity to the world of charting:

When you understand the charts, you understand life.

In fact, since I have become a chartist, I have achieved a better understanding of life.

Learning to surf goes something this. First, you have to confront your fear of big waves and sharks. Then you have to be prepared to look really incompetent (a foam board doesn't help!). Next you must have the courage to stand up and try. The reality is that most people never learn a new physical activity once they become an adult, especially one that involves danger.

So picture this: I am paddling hard, trying to reach the waves. In the process, I get dumped about a million times just trying to get past the rip. And all of this happens while I am still lying flat on the board. Then, when I get out to where the waves begin, I see all these really good surfers who are half my age and straightaway am feeling intimidated. A big wave finally comes along and I paddle like crazy and try to remember everything I have been taught (three lessons from the surf school) and I don't even get halfway up before I realise I am no longer on my board. So, I struggle back onto my board and paddle like crazy again.

The next few times I make minimal progress. On about my fourth attempt I manage to catch a wave and I stand for about a nanosecond. This is a good feeling, but I look back at the

163

smug teenage boys and they're giving me the 'you're so feeble' look. Then I am paddling out again. This goes on for a while—sometimes I stand up for a moment and mostly I just fall off.

After about an hour and a half I start to get a little weary. Just as I think I should probably take the rented board back to the surf shop, I catch a perfect wave, and I ride it all the way into shore. I am elated and suddenly understand why people are crazy about this sport.

Here is why learning to surf is like trading (which is just like life):

↳ Waves are like stock charts

↳ Traders are like surfers.

Surfers talk about the perfect wave. The real diehards will go half-way around the world to find them, often risking their lives on reefs and rips. Risking money is the closest thing the average trader gets to risking life. When you decide to trade you are paddling fast trying to catch that wave.

The good surfers wait in exactly the right position and only take the waves that will give them the longest run. They are alert to the fact that the waves change and you need to re-position yourself to keep finding the best waves. These guys understand that waves move in cycles, yet they are attuned enough to realise that these cycles also change. Good surfers also know that a run will not last forever and they understand the precise moment to jump off and abandon a wave that doesn't have momentum. Others, like myself, are so impatient to get up in the beginning that they'll throw themselves at anything that moves.

It is normal for new traders to try and jump on any trade that comes along. But the longer you trade, the better you get, the more selective your trade choices, and the more certainty you will feel when you take a trade.

Beginning something new always involves a learning curve. If you are moving from stock trading to CFD trading, be prepared for this process. The learning curve is a lot like the chart of a stock. At the beginning, it doesn't seem like any progress is being made. Then, a small breakthrough occurs. You continue to make progress and feel like you've turned a corner, but for every four good waves, you take one that makes you remember your are truly pathetic at this.

Sound familiar? This is typical of the early stages of a new uptrend. Some people give up when this happens—'it is too hard, I'll never be any good at this,' is what we have all said at some time in our lives. The 'tech bubble' no doubt flushed out a lot of the lilly-livered traders who didn't understand that if they wanted to be really good at something it was going to take effort and disappointment, especially at the beginning.

The key to becoming a good surfer, a good CFD trader, or a good 'anything', is to understand the natural order of life. A new endeavour will always take more effort and even the most skilled can take a fall. Now, whenever I think about taking up a new activity or learning a new skill, I have no fear about struggling to be good. I know that beginnings will, and should be, about making mistakes. It is a slow, steady progress that gives me the staying power to keep on going.

From Chapter 1 you will recall that, when I first became involved in technical analysis, I was obsessed with the most complicated and mysterious forms of analysis. Now, eight years into a passionate obsession with the art, I only look at the price action itself and try and apply the concept of a natural order of things—new uptrends should start slowly and steadily and fast uptrends will eventually lead to fast corrections. Central to this philosophy is the view that charts (and life) are inevitably a cycle, so don't fight it.

Psychology Checklist

During my career as an analyst and writer I have had the fortune to interview some very successful large-scale traders. These big swingers never get complacent. They are always standing in the fire. The difference between them and the average punter is their ability to manage the intensity of this experience.

There will always be moments when you get too confident, and be tempted to take a trade with too much risk, hold a losing position for too long or just do something that is plain stupid. Trading involves being eternally vigilant to the emotional pitfalls. There is no way of teaching new traders how to avoid these pitfalls until they have experienced a losing trade for themselves. It's like a child putting their hand in a fire—you never quite believe it will burn until it does. And unfortunately, for most of us, it takes more than one bad experience to put us on the right track to good discipline.

Despite this, you can educate and prepare yourself to deal with this experience. For new CFD traders who want to cut some corners on the hard road to successful trading here are some pointers for the journey:

1   **Expect to lose some money; everyone does it.**
    Losing is winning—a great paradox of trading.
    Nothing improves your strategy more than losing cash.

2   **Practise discipline in other areas of your life.**
    Discipline in life equals discipline in trading. The stress of trading needs a physical outlet. Exercise is a way to practise discipline and let off steam.

3   **No-one else knows best.** The most money you will ever lose in trading will probably be because you listened to someone else's opinions. Keep your own counsel and avoid the external noise.

4   **Be brave.** Successful traders don't pussy-foot their way to big rewards. Put yourself on the line, it's the only way to improve.

5   **Take responsibility.** Greed turns us into idiots. When you stuff up, your first response will be to blame someone or something else. Blame will only keep you stuck in the past, and that's loser land.

6   **Ask lots of questions.** When you need to know something—ask. Your CFD account manager has heard every dumb question possible.

7   **Don't get tricky until you know the basics.** CFDs are a new product, so make sure you understand the mechanics by starting with small trades. That goes for your trading strategy as well.

8   **Don't drop the ball when you lose.** When you lose money, your first instinct is to get even. When you lose a lot of money your initial reaction will be to give up completely. Think about it—autobiographies are usually stories about losers who just kept trying.

9   **Share the pain.** Get some trading mates. Join a trading club or the ATAA (Australian Technical Analysts Association). Human contact will help your self esteem when you lose money and open your mind to new trading ideas.

10 **Write a business plan.** It's hard to find the end of the road if it's not on your map. Write down your trading goals with the same degree of stringency as a business plan. This will help you focus and stimulate those unseen universal forces which help to make dreams come true.

PERSONAL PERFORMANCE CHART

It is a well-known fact that the actual returns of investing in a managed fund are a lot lower than the recorded annual returns of the fund. This is because of a phenomenon called 'fund rotation'. Investors are attracted to buy into funds when the fund managers returns are at their highest and sell out of a fund when it is showing low returns. This year's best performing fund becomes next year's mediocre performer, or even loser, and vice versa.

The result of investors jumping from one fund to another is the realisation of very low returns. When you trade for yourself, you are, in effect, a fund manager. There are lessons to be learnt about your own trading by understanding 'fund rotation'.

Success Cycles

There are two factors at play here. The first is the cyclical nature of life. The core of our existence is based on cycles that structure the natural order of things—for example, seasons and moon phases. The very nature of life is that reality shifts beneath us, no matter what we do to control it. Our emotional responses reflect these natural processes.

Secondly, highs create lows and, in turn, lows create highs. This is because successful trading breeds recklessness, while the opposite—losing money—can force us to get smart.

Zeal Leads to Downfall

Having a series of winning trades followed by a large losing trade is a common experience. It is the dose of reality that hits lucky beginners, but it can happen at any time in your trading career.

Success brings overconfidence and this can destroy returns. The bursting of the 'tech bubble' came on the heels of many new investors entering the market via the first Telstra offering. I remember from my days as a futures broker a new trader telling me he was keen to start trading futures because he was so successful at stocks. When I asked him what stocks he had traded, he mentioned a large holding in Telstra. Back in 1998 I suspect many investors thought they were successful investors just because they held Telstra stocks. Needless to say his futures trading career was short.

When the new technology stocks started to garner media attention and draw in amateur traders who had no more experience than owning Telstra, the scene was set for some reckless trading and big losses.

Lessons Learned

Investors in managed funds will exit a fund with weak returns and swap to the best-performing fund. They leave a fund as the bottom of a wave gathers momentum and join another at the crest of a wave that is about to fall. Private investing is the same. Small investors give up when their easy pickings turn into painful losses. Big losses can either drive you to leave the market altogether or inspire you to get a better trading strategy.

A better trading strategy means finding an approach to the market where you have watertight entry and exit rules with a proven high probability of success in the past. However, even with a good strategy in hand, the best traders can flout their system and fly on the new wings of recent success. This happens to everybody at some time.

Understanding is Most of the Battle

The most important aspect of dealing with the cyclical nature of trading is to understand the psychological nature of this problem. People often say that awareness is nine tenths of overcoming a bad habit.

Being aware that a large or long winning streak is often followed by poor trading decisions which will make a major difference to your trading performance.

Good Practice

There are five steps that can help you overcome the tendency to give back your winnings:

1   After a successful run, realise your next trading decision is more likely to be a reckless one.

2   Monitor your success—charting it can highlight when you are on the verge of making a 'correction' to your profits.

3   Stick to your rules faultlessly.

4   Focus on your returns and not your flair for picking entries and exits.

5   Remind yourself there are no gurus, just some traders who are more disciplined than others.

Most traders at some time have experienced the overconfidence that can lead to losses. Remember this is a natural human reaction and becoming aware of it is more than many traders can expect in their trading experience.

Charting Your Returns

Keeping records of your trading activity is part of being a disciplined trader. Turning this data into a personal performance chart can highlight when you may be heading for a fall. In the same way that an overheated market will eventually suffer a sell-off, your trading returns are also subject to a cyclical process.

When you start trading or begin to trade with a new strategy you can expect mixed results and the kind of bottoming patterns you see on stock charts, such as double or triple bottoms or a head and shoulders pattern. Small amounts of progress may be followed by losses of equal size. In some ways this is the best scenario for a beginner. It means you are experiencing the idea of loss in the early stages of your career.

As your trading improves you can expect the winning periods to last longer and the losses to be more limited and more manageable. As your profits increase you could then enter a phase where your winning system stops working or an element of overconfidence starts to hinder your trading success. This is the time to pull back, check your system, re-evaluate your trading business plan and even stop trading for a while. Some traders even run a moving average over their trading results in order to identify an early warning sign of bad performance.

DESERVING THE DOLLARS

There is a theory in the markets that says we receive from our trading efforts what we subconsciously think we deserve. If you have a dream to be making $1,000,000 from your share portfolio a year, and you are lucky to make $10,000, then it's time you checked the dark persona within.

Too Good to be True

The idea of making what you deserve is probably the reason why beginner's luck is an ephemeral experience. Often when new traders make an easy profit, their brains literally double-take and they say to themselves, 'this is too good to be true'. In time they are proved right.

No matter what stage of your trading career, the sense of taking what you think you deserve is in the background, cutting your profits short and ignoring the big winners.

Analysis Paralysis

How do we analyse a share correctly and then watch it take a ride without being on board? Most people think the most significant way to improve their trading performance is by making more effort in the form of study. This might be true initially but, after a certain level of knowledge is gained, further study can work against us. Being blinded by science is a common pitfall for new technical traders. It is important to realise that the hardest battle for the trader is the battle with their own limiting beliefs.

Subconscious Reality

Our subconscious reality is the seed that grows our external world. Subconscious thoughts constantly direct decisions and manifest in the reality of existence. If you are reckless with your money generally, then your trading will follow the same theme. The biggest problem with subconscious reality is its insidiousness. Without conscious awareness it is a force that can sabotage even the best efforts.

Identifying and Controlling Your Subconscious Reality

The first task is to acknowledge this inner voice by identifying the thought process involved in making a bad trading decision. My own negative inner voice works something like this: I find a potential trade and subconsciously refer to recent trades I have taken that have not moved as quickly as I had hoped. I then assume this stock will probably perform in the same manner. I check the chart again and overlay this negative thought, looking for any indications that the share might not be a good buy. I then watch the price action and, like many stocks that have recently made a break from important resistance, there is indeed a pause in the uptrend and often a pullback. Over the course of the next few days the stock leaps higher and runs away without me.

Acknowledging this tendency to procrastinate over a potential trading opportunity has had a dramatic effect on my bottom line. Analyse your last few bad trades. Try and identify a pattern of negative subconscious thought patterns.

Damage Control Strategies

Getting a System

The first strategy is to have a strategy. Obviously this needs to be one with a high probability of success. If you are using a trading approach and you have no idea how successful it is in the real world, and more particularly on the share CFDs you want to trade, then there is more opportunity for your subconscious to direct your trading.

A trading approach that you have personally researched and proven to be successful will not just give you a winning strategy but also prime your subconscious for success.

Self Helping

I am surprised by the number of successful traders I have interviewed who subscribe to self-help books. Successful trading is as much a journey into knowing yourself as learning to make the right trading decisions. Every great idea started as just a thought, so visualising yourself as a successful trader is one of the most powerful ways to re-program your subconscious.

True Grit

When you watch Hollywood's depiction of Wall Street traders they are invariably ruthless and hard. While this might seem like just another stereotype, there is something to be said for adopting this mental attitude when it comes to investing in shares. An unwavering focus on your strategy, the wherewithal to stick to your analysis, no matter what others around you are saying, and the unshakeable commitment to follow through are all the hallmarks of the successful trader.

In a nutshell, a good trader will confront the inner battle with true grit.

One of the first things to change in your thinking is your attitude to the learning process. There are very few wrong calls in the world of charting. The beauty of the trade is truly in the eyes of the beholder. What I see may be different to the next technical analyst, but both of us can be right when we trade with our own agendas. Setting a realistic financial goal from trading is one of the best ways to focus your subconscious mind on a positive outcome. Negative inner thoughts can never be fully eradicated. However becoming aware of limiting beliefs and acting consciously to acknowledge and dismiss them can transform your trading.

INDEX

—checklist 165-166
—damage control 172-173
put option 28, 29

QBE Insurance Limited 77

rally 67, 70, 74
real-time trading 53
reduced capital outlay 56
Reserve Bank of Australia
(RBA) 21, 49
resistance 66, 68, 79, 90-98,
120, 133-135
resource companies 63
retracements 66, 79-81,
133-135
reversals 67, 68, 72, 83-90
rights issues 22
Rio Tinto Limited 63, 75
risk 4, 50-51, 54
rollover 24, 26, 31
round numbers 66, 91

S&P/ASX 200 24, 25
sales data 66
sector trading 17, 30, 65,
142-143
Securities and Exchange
Commission (SEC) 7
segregated funds account 32
sell and hold 152-153
September 11, 2001 75,
146-147, 149
shareholder benefits 22
shares 29-31, 153

Share Price Index (SPI) 23,
24, 26
share trading, traditional 56,
61, 64
'short covering' 72
short position 19, 22, 28,
44-46, 70
short-term market analysis
61-124, 136-139
sideways trading 68
slippage 58-59
Solution 6 Holdings Limited
63
spike 84
spread betting 30-31, 33, 48
spreads 29, 35-37, 47-48
—cost impact 36-37
—profitability 37
—size 35-36
spread size 38, 63
stalking the market 64-65
stamp duty 17, 29, 46
standardised contracts 23
Stanwell Tops 10-12
stock splits 22
stop-entry order 58
stop-loss 7, 52, 59, 89, 90, 96,
102, 107, 115, 137, 139,
161-162
—Fibonacci 115-118
—orders 40, 58, 60, 61
—using support and
resistance 120-121
—trailing 115-124
—using gaps 119-121